KAR GUYS

Mehdi Roufougar

BALBOA.
PRESS

A DIVISION OF HAY HOUSE

Balboa Press books may be ordered through booksellers or by contacting:

Balboa Press
A Division of Hay House
1663 Liberty Drive
Bloomington, IN 47403
www.balboapress.com
1-(877) 407-4847

Because of the dynamic nature of the Internet, any web addresses or links contained in this book may have changed since publication and may no longer be valid. The views expressed in this work are solely those of the author and do not necessarily reflect the views of the publisher, and the publisher hereby disclaims any responsibility for them.

The author of this book does not dispense medical advice or prescribe the use of any technique as a form of treatment for physical, emotional, or medical problems without the advice of a physician, either directly or indirectly. The intent of the author is only to offer information of a general nature to help you in your quest for emotional and spiritual well-being. In the event you use any of the information in this book for yourself, which is your constitutional right, the author and the publisher assume no responsibility for your actions.

Any people depicted in stock imagery provided by Thinkstock are models, and such images are being used for illustrative purposes only.
Certain stock imagery © Thinkstock.
Editor: A-1 Editing Service LLC
Final editing by: Amy Rivera
Cover design by: Perris valley Printing

Printed in the United States of America.

ISBN: 978-1-4525-7171-3 (sc)
ISBN: 978-1-4525-7172-0 (e)

Balboa Press rev. date: 5/15/2013

Contents

Chapter one

DEALERS

"Over 99 percent of car dealers give the rest a bad name."

DISHONEST DEALERS, GENERAL MANAGERS, SALES MANAGERS and closers are the reason this book was written.

Every finger pointing, name calling and bad mouthing is directed only at them and it is unfortunate that they out number the honest ones on the scale of "too many to one."

This book was not written with the intention of putting the writers name on the authors' lists, it was not written to make him famous among the car guys or car dealership employees and it was not written to educate consumers about purchasing vehicles or teaching the salesmen how to sell cars.

It was written to show the different tricks that crooked dealers have been using to steal time and money from their salesmen/women, fleet, internet and finance managers in the name of "commission."

For decades these con artists have for their own benefit directly or indirectly been using their general managers, desk men, used car managers, closers and even their parts and service departments to screw the salespeople out of the real commission that they were promised at the time of their employment.

There has been no limit to their unfair business practices and there is no reason to believe that they will stop their criminal acts now.

With the internet being an important selling source of automobiles these days, so many auto manufactures and car dealers are cutting each others' throats to capture a chunk of the market and that even would make it harder for the car salespeople to make their living and they do not see any light at the end of the tunnel.

Those of you who have worked for any amount of time in car dealerships as a commission salesperson, fleet, internet, finance and sales manager, general sales manager or even general manager already know that car dealers are the biggest slave drivers out there.

It is ok for these crooked assholes to make several hundred thousand dollars every month but if their salespeople make a few dollars more than the normal average for a couple of months in a row, they will raise the pack or change their pay plans in order to "control" their salespeople's income.

These selfish lazy weasels are so used to manipulating people for their own benefit that by now, being dishonest with their sales people seems very normal and standard in their corrupted industry and if anyone does not go along with their unfair and unlawful programs, his/her dismissal from the dealership is guaranteed.

Car dealers have no appreciation for anybody and it doesn't matter what position their targets hold.

All it takes to set them off is for some one to say something that they don't like to hear. It doesn't make any difference if that someone is a porter, salesman, closer, fleet, finance or sales manager. He/she can be part, service, body shop employee or even their general manager. Dealers do not want to hear backtalk of any kind. They do the talking and you do the listening. They do not work you do the work for them and you do it without "ifs ands or buts."

To them you are just a number and your number is up as soon as they feel that you are not making them enough money. What you have done for them in the past is history. They are firm believers of "what have you done for me lately?"

They do not give a shit about your position or number of years that you have put in at their dealerships and the sad thing about it is that their general managers, sales managers and closers know all of this but they still take the assholes' side and follow his/her orders to screw others.

Some of the dealers are known as the "lucky sperm" and they inherited the dealership from their parents. There are some who are married to the owners' daughter and became a member of the management team and later on took over the dealership.

You will find a few who started with a partner and one partner screwed the other and took over the dealership. There are also many who started as a wholesaler with a couple of vehicles and kept selling until they changed the chicken shit to chicken salad and became car dealers.

You may also find some athletes, lawyers, doctors, movie stars or outside business people with the money who have invested in car dealerships without being known as a car dealer. They are called absent dealers and usually have a general manager to run their dealership for them but just like any good businessman they know where every dollar of the profit is coming from.

Overall dishonest dealers forget who they are and how they got there but they all have one thing in common and that is screwing anyone and everyone.

"Salespeople" in this book refers to car salesmen/women, fleet, internet, and finance managers. Although some of these salespeople carry the management title but in reality they do not manage anything or anyone except their own paychecks.

Making money is getting harder and harder for the salespeople and dealers keep putting more and more pressure and making them work harder and put in more hours with less pay.

Some salespeople hear that the grass is greener on the other side of the fence and after getting screwed several times by their dealer, come to believe that the other dealer is more honest and will not steal from them as much or may even have a better pay plan.

They keep moving from one dealer to another to make a better living but very soon they find out that the grass on the other side is not greener and the other dealer is as crooked and kinky as the previous asshole and it was all a matter of false hope.

After going from one dealer to another so many times they finally give up and accept the fact that dishonest dealers are all the same shit in different toilets.

Anywhere they go the same thing is happening, so might as well stay at the same corrupted toilet and get used to it.

I say it just like it is. I know that few readers may get offended or be put off by using profanity or some of the expressions that are considered crude by the polite society.

My objective is to utilize the syntax and conversational style found in most of the car dealerships themselves.

Certain words and phrases have been used in this book for better or worse as the part of the life of the employees, managers, and owners of the dealerships and make readers familiar with the situation and those having their eyes opened for the first time in the dealerships. A realistic view of attitudes and what is really happening in the dealerships are encountered here.

My anger is apparent. I am as angry as anyone who has experienced the grossly unfair practices of the auto sales industries' business or anyone encountering the truth for the first time can.

My style is offensive and I intend to wake up all those who accept the situations and make them free themselves from being used as slaves from the selfish, dishonest, kinky and crooked car dealers.

What you are about to read is the truth, the whole truth, and nothing but the truth without any exaggeration or bullshit.

Car salespeople do not know what to do, who to turn to or where to go to protect themselves from getting screwed by dealers, manufactures, or some selfish "lookie loos" who are not really customers but want to waste the salespeople's time for their own stupid pleasure and curiosity.

Raising pack, flooding floor, open floor policy, stealing from the front end gross of the salesmen deals, hidden packs, holding commissions on the deals, inflating the repair cost of the used vehicles, forcing salespeople to spend hours of their time in daily or weekly repetitive sales meetings, making them spend their time on the CSI (customer satisfaction index), forcing them to stay in the BDC (business development center) without compensation are some of the kinky and unfair business practices that most of the car and RV dealers are using in their dealerships to screw their salespeople out of their time and money.

Again this book only refers to dishonest car dealers, general managers, deskmen and closers. If you are one of the few of the honest examples of the above who has not in any way screwed his/her sales people out of their fair share of commission or time and you are a firm believer of what is fair and correct for everybody, I admire you and I take my hat off to you. You are really one of a kind.

There are many laws, rules and regulations to protect consumers, dealers and manufactures, but unfortunately there really are no laws or regulations to protect commissioned car salespeople from getting screwed by those same dealers because dishonest dealers hide their documents from their employees and it is very hard for the salespeople to prove that dealers have been cheating them out of their real fair share of commissions.

We all know that the labor department cannot go after a person who wastes several hours of a salesman time. Nor will they take action against car manufactures on the salesmen behalf, because salespeople are not the manufacturers direct employees although car manufacturers do have a lot of indirect influences that they can use to push their franchise car dealers to punish anyone of the salespeople.

I have sold a lot of vehicles in my life as a car salesman, fleet and internet manager and I have typed thousands of deals as a finance manager. I have had my share of good and bad days, real customers and jack offs and I was not surprised to see that the jack offs always outnumber the real buyers.

There have been times that I made over two thousand dollars in two hours and there were times that I did not make even one dollar in a week but that is not the subjects of this book.

For the last several years I have been asking myself, why do car salespeople let the dealers, manufacturers or these wanna-be customers or in plain English language "jack offs" screw them left and right out of time and money? Why do the salespeople let themselves be used as slaves or cheap laborers? Why do they let these assholes walk all over them without paying anything and get away with it? Why is a car sales person's time seen as worthless to the car dealers, consumers and car manufactures?

I realized that we salesmen/women, fleet and internet managers are the ones who are guilty of letting these crooked assholes to walk all over us.

Car manufacturers keep advertising come and test drive our new vehicles. Car dealers keep advertising in gimmicky ways to bring customers to their doors and expect their salesmen to switch them from the loss leaders to another vehicle or change their mind from purchase to lease.

There should be no excuse for dealers to make their salesmen unlock their vehicles in the mornings or lock them at nights or to wash the sold units after hours.

These are the porters' jobs and if car dealers are too cheap to pay their porters to open and lock their vehicles or pay a little overtime to their porters to stay and wash the sold units after hours they should wash their own fucking vehicles or get their ass kissing sales managers or their puppet general managers to do that.

It is only fair that manufacturers pay every salesperson for the time that they are forced to spend in the "ride and drives" instead of a cup of coffee and donut or a sandwich and soda. They should also take the "completely satisfied" bullshit out of their fucking surveys knowing that the salesmen have no authority to stop finance, service or part departments from the high pressures that they put on customers to sell them all kinds of unnecessary repairs and other garbage in order to make their own fucking commissions.

Manufacturers are not the salesmen employers. They do not help or protect salesmen in any way and if there should be any CSI, it should be for the dealers not the salesmen. Vehicles belong to the car dealers so dealers or their general managers should call customers and thank them for their business. After all they are the dealer's customers not the salespeople.

If manufacturers run a "test drive" advertisements for their new vehicle they should have a designated area for the test drives to take place. Also they should pay their own employees to take customers for the drive, or pay the car salesmen something from their own pockets to demo their new vehicles otherwise, consumers can spend a few dollars and rent the fucking vehicles to see how they drive instead of going to car lots and waste the car salesmen's time.

Commissioned car salesmen/women are not getting paid based on the number of test drives, write ups, unlocking cars in the morning and locking them at night or blowing up balloons. They are not getting paid for being certified, how good their CSI is or the time that they spend in the BDC rooms, sales meetings and ride and drives nor for the times that they spend on the phone kissing customers' asses and begging them to say "we are completely satisfied" for the fucking dealer to get the credit.

Car manufacturers do not give a shit about the salespeople. Car dealers are using salespeople just like slaves and consumers think that it is the car salespeople's job and they are getting paid to explain the fixtures and features of vehicles.

Consumers expect the salesmen to take them on demo rides just because they want to know about the horse power, torque, safety and most of all how these vehicles drive.

We all know that manufacturers have been forcing their franchise dealers to send their salespersons to go on ride and drives and spending hours studying the owners manuals to be introduced to their new vehicles and become certified without paying them anything but a cup of coffee and donut that they call it continental breakfast or a cold cut and soda called lunch.

Another word, several hours of car salespeople time is worth about two to three dollars to the car manufacturers. This does not even take into the account that some of these salespeople burn more than $15 in gas to attend these stupid ride & drives bullshit. Most of the salespeople have to go to these stupid ride and drives on their off shifts or on the days that they are off without getting pay for their times.

We also know that car manufacturers have been indirectly forcing their franchise dealers to push their salespeople to spend time in the BDC or the follow up rooms without compensation and punish them for the low CSI.

It is very obvious that society has no respect for car salesmen. Some jack asses do not want the salesmen to approach them when they go to car lots and some selfish, rude and even more asshole ones do not even shake hands with the car salesmen.

It has been proven that customers have changed from one salesperson to another for thirty dollars less on the price after wasting three or four hours of the initial salesmans' time without giving him or her a chance to try to match the price or payments.

We experience it all the time, we see it all the time, we feel it all the time and we bitch and complain about it all the time but we haven't done anything to stop it.

As far as I know, we can complain and bitch all we want, they do not give a shit and will keep doing what they have been doing for the last several decades and believe it or not they will keep screwing us more and more.

If they hear you complain they call you an OBT (on board terrorist) or refer to you as a whiner, complainer, bad apple and poison. They will tell you straight up "if you do not like it, get the hell out." You are employed at will and that means we can do what we want. We can raise the pack at any time, we can change the pay plan at any time and we can discharge you at will.

Some of these con artists even force you to waive your rights to a trial by the jury and accept the arbitration just in case something happens later on during your employment with them.

The funny thing is they call it voluntary but if you take a look at their employment application you'll see that your signature automatically commits you to their unfair arbitration rules.

They know that there are a lot more chances to fool one arbitrator than twelve members of the jury when at least eleven of them have been fucked by a dealer already.

Any way you look at it, It is not possible to fight them on an individual basis to get our fair share of commission because these assholes do not believe in what is fair and correct for everybody.

The point that I am trying to make to the car dealers is very simple, "pay your commissioned employees what they were promised at the time of their employment and take your hands out of their pockets."

If your pay plan says 20% of the profit after the pack, pay them the real 20%. Do not inflate the repair cost, do not steal from their front end gross and do not add hidden packs to the cost to reduce the commission that they deserve and screw them on the real pay plan that you promised them at the time of employment.

Don't charge $295 for an oil change on a used four cylinder vehicle in the deal and hide it from your salesmen. That is not your real cost.

You are not paying your mechanics $100 per hour labor that you are charging to the deals and replacing a battery does not take three hours labor that you claim.

Real cost for an after market alarm is not $325 or even 1/3rd of that. Why do you pack the cost to your finance managers over $200?

Reconditioning cost to a ten month old vehicle which has less than 11000 miles with no body damage still 100% under the manufacture warranty cannot be $2995.

What can you possibly do to a vehicle of this type that costs so much? This is not even including the several hundred dollars regular pack that the dealer has already.

A few scumbag dealers have no shame to con their salesmen/women with an extra pack for the sake of the six month power train warranty on their used vehicles. This comes in addition to their regular pack knowing that most of their used vehicles have the remaining of power train warranty from the manufacturers already.

These con artists do not have the balls to tell their salespeople at the time of their employment how much their real pack is. They use different tricks to add to their real cost and rip off their salespeople.

There is an old saying "to get along, go along" but this rule does not apply when you are working for dishonest car dealers. They steal from you any chance they get just like a thief and there is no way that you can get along or go along with thieves unless you become a thief too.

Society thinks car salesmen are crooks. They do not know that salespeople are just the middlemen with no authority whatsoever in the dealerships.

Manufacturers want the salespeople to say their new vehicles are better than others and salespeople relay that to the customers. They want the salesmen to tell customers that their certified used vehicles have been through 150 point inspections and the salesman knowing that the fucking vehicle has not even seen three inspections by the service department has to convince the customer about the 150 point bullshit inspections.

Car dealers want their salesmen to convince consumers that they are getting the best deal and the salesmen in turn relay that to the customers.

Most salespeople do not like to mislead customers and some are so new to the business (green peas) that they do not even know what is happening. Dealers and manufacturers force them to do that though it is the salespeople who get all of the blame.

Car salesmen are the ones who do not get any respect from the society. Crooked dealers, their general managers, sales managers and closers who coach their salesmen do not have to worry about that.

This book is for those ass kissing "closers" who can rarely keep a job in one dealership and keep going from one dealer to another like monkeys hopping trees. They work at one place for a short time and try to make the salesmen believe that they are making them money.

These compulsive liars have no balls and no authority whatsoever to prevent car dealers from screwing their salesmen, but they act like they are the boss. In fact they like to be called "boss" by the salesmen or saleswomen when they are being introduced to the customers to close deals.

Some of them cannot even close a fucking door but they keep putting their salesmen down and blame them for their own weakness of not closing deals.

They make fun of the salesmen and treat them like they are stupid and do not know anything and look down on them. They make jokes about their nationality, religion, accent and even their skin colors.

How easily these jackasses forget that they too were salesmen once and were being treated like shit themselves. Now instead of helping the salesmen, they are just puppets for the dealers.

This book is for those "deskmen" who keep sucking up to their bosses because of the big paychecks that the salespeople are making for them. Most of them do not have a college degree and some do not even have a high school diploma yet car dealers call them "sales managers."

Deskmen's incomes depend 100% on the salespeople's production but since their boss has given them the position the boss makes them think that he is being very generous to them and for that reason wants them to cover up for his fraudulent acts and these ass kissers can't or won't stand up to him/her for what is fair for everybody.

Deskmen also like to be called "boss" and they do not want to accept that they are just another peon in the dealerships.

This book is for the general sales managers who really are not authorized to do anything without checking with their general managers or the owners. I haven't figured out why car dealers even have a general sales manager as they don't do any more work and have no more authority than the deskmen anyway.

And, this book is for those puppet general managers who are making too much money with just a few hours work. They make an average of over one to several hundred dollars per hour for what they really do (depending on the dealership) so they must dance to whatever music the owners are playing. They completely become puppets to their bosses.

These master thieves would kill to put a smile on their bosses face and would not hesitate to screw customers in the parts, service, sales, finance and the body shop in order to make more money for the owner.

They also do not hesitate to cheat any employee at any time and will not hesitate to force their management to do something unethical to keep the money flowing and make their owners happy.

The bottom line is, if their boss is happy they are happy otherwise they will have long faces and want to take it out on their sales team.

I remember one of my general sales managers saying "shit always rolls down from the top." He would repeat that in the sales meetings every time that business was slow.

These master thieves are more loyal to their bosses than a republican senator to the republican party, a democrat congressman to the democrat party and any general to the president because based on their education and number of hours that they really work they make more money than congressmen, senators, generals and even the president without having college degree and sometimes even a high school diploma.

Car dealers have several managers in their dealerships. In fact they have so many that sometimes it seems that managers are running out of the dealerships' asses. These crooks give away management titles left and right to confuse customers and fool their own employees.

Lots of them have a general manager and a general sales manager, an executive manager, several sales managers (deskmen) two or more finance managers, one or more fleet or internet managers, BDC manager, used car manager, service manager, parts manager, body shop manager, collection manager, business manager, office manager, accounts payable/receivable manager. I do not know why they do not call their head porters, "porter manager?"

As kinky as these crooks are, even their closers title on the business cards reads "assistant sales manager." They even make the closers believe that they are some kind of managers too.

It just does not make any sense that they have changed the name of "used cars" to "previously owned vehicles" but their used car manager is still called used car manager not "previously owned vehicle manager."

What is amazing is that in most cases none of these managers have been through any management school or have taken any management course or training in their life and some of these managers do not manage anyone or anything except their own paychecks. Fleet, internet and finance managers are among them. If fleet or internet managers do not sell any vehicle or finance managers do not sell warranty, alarm, gap, lo jack and other items in the back end of the deals they are not issued a paycheck.

Car dealers have a habit of brain washing their general managers, general sales managers, sales managers and closers by having them believe that the dealer makes money for the managers, they in turn want these managers to brainwash the salespeople with the idea that they are making money because of the car dealer' generosity to give them the opportunity to work in his/her dealership.

Their managers are so happy to have been given a management title and it goes to their heads so fast that they forget about everything else.

For the most part lots of them do not even care about the money, they are just so proud to be called managers.

Those who have never been managers before love to carry the title with them so much that they continuously brag about it and make sure that their friends, neighbors and family members know it.

These assholes get so absorbed in their title that they forget who they are and what they are supposed to manage.

Con artist dealers are giving these people management titles without sending them to take any management courses or training in a college, university or trade school. They just learn how to screw others from their crooked bosses.

Dealers are afraid to have educated managers managing their dealerships and often fear sending their managers to take one or two courses in management at a college or university as such education would make them less vulnerable to their egotistical ignorance.

They force their salesmen to go to specific training to become familiar with new vehicles and become "certified" for two reasons. First, their franchise manufacturers force them to and the second, it does not cost them any money however, getting their managers educated is a big no-no to them.

Sales managers and closers are especially guilty of acting like they are making money for the salesmen. They seem to believe that they are doing the salesmen a big favor by giving them the opportunity to make money. But just to refresh these sales managers' memories, if salesmen do not sell there would be no paychecks for closers or the sales managers.

Sales managers are not doing salesmen any favor by hiring them, they need salesmen and they must have them to sell their vehicles because again there would be no paychecks for them if salesmen do not sell vehicles.

Salesmen/women are the engine of every car dealership. They are the reason for every dollar profit that is made in the front and back end of deals. They are feeding finance managers, sales managers, general sales managers and a huge portion of general managers and most of a car dealers' income is dependent on the salesmen productions.

Manufacturers do not exist without car salesmen. They can make the best and safest vehicle in the world but if salesmen don't sell them it's all over for them.

To keep the manufacturers open and producing, they must sell their products to their franchise dealers. To keep car dealerships open and producing, they must have sales teams. Sales teams consist of closers, deskmen, fleet, internet, finance managers, and salesmen/women.

Salesmans' job is to make customers fall in love with the vehicle and get them to come inside. We all know that vehicles are being sold outside but deals are being made inside. As a result, the salesman must sell himself first and then convince the customer to come inside to make the deal.

One of the sales managers' jobs is to desk the deal. To do that, they usually get their sharpies out and write some big numbers on the four squares (work sheets).

In "straight sale" stores, salesmen show that to the customer. After two or three rounds of this where the sales manager comes up with a number and the customer agrees, the salesman closes the deal. In the T - O (turn over) stores, sales manager will get the closer to close the deal with the same tactic.

When the deal is closed and the shaking of hands are done the deal is sent to the finance manager to sell the garbage that car dealers want him/her to sell.

The reality is, the whole process of selling vehicles always starts with the car salesmen.

If they do not sell themselves and do not use their sales talent to convince the customers to come inside and make a deal, sales managers would never desk, closers would never close and finance managers would never be able to sell their back end bullshit.

As a result, car dealers would not move their units and if dealers do not sell their inventories, manufactures have no way to sell their products. A lack of sales means laying off employees and shutting down car manufacturers.

No matter what kind of bullshit these con artists tell you, making the deal always starts with salesmen/women, they are the ones who are making it happen.

Salesmen are the keys to the units that are being sold and no dealership can survive without them. I also need to add something here for the finance managers.

It is unfortunate that most finance managers do not have a good attitude toward salesmen especially if the deal that they are going to type is a cash deal, option contract or the customer has foreign name or some special occupation.

They think that the salesman went to India, Pakistan, the Middle East, or the Far East on purpose to bring Mr. Patel, Abdul, Kareem, Nguyen, Tran, Chang or Singh to America to sell them a vehicle just to piss that finance manager off.

They think salesmen are telling the customers to write a check for the total price of the vehicle including tax and license ahead of time to block the finance managers from selling their garbage or the salesman called this engineer, doctor or lawyer that are harder to sell to than the blue collar lay downs on his follow up list just to make the life more difficult for the finance manager and bring down his/her back end gross average.

Most finance managers already have such a negative attitude toward foreign born people or even toward educated customers, cash buyers or option financing that they do not even try to sell something.

They get so frustrated just by looking at names or at a customers profession or cash deals that they forget the old saying "if you don't ask, you don't get." They do not pitch and do not try to sell anything but blame the sales person for the ways that customers are purchasing, or for the customers' nationality and profession.

As far as I am concerned, they can sit in their little offices and play with their own dicks or pussies all day long, they do not have a chance to take a shot at a customer to sell their crap unless the salesman sell the vehicle and that customer sits in front of them.

Some of the finance managers are so spoiled that they expect their sales managers to steal a chunk of the front end gross of the salesperson and give it to them for loading customers information in the computer and type the deal.

If you have noticed, I have been calling the items that finance managers sell in the back end of the deals "garbage" for obvious reasons. Some of these items like gap insurance, warranty and lo jack are not garbage. In fact they may become useful to the customers later, but a lot of greedy car dealers push their finance managers to make as much profit on any one of these items and sell them at such an expensive rate that it makes the extras look like they are not worth the price and are in fact garbage.

Usually smart customers do not lay down for those programs and they buy them outside and not from the dealers. Now let's see how sales managers make their living.

They have to work very hard and kiss a lot of asses and buy a lot of breakfasts and lunches for their bosses to become desk men. Dealers call them "sales managers."

When they get that job they must continue kissing asses to keep it because they do not want to lose those big paychecks that the salespeople are making for them.

Right away they forget who is making them the money and become the "puppets" for their general managers and the owners of the dealership. They would do anything to keep their bosses happy and dance to any kind of music that the bosses play.

Usually car dealers have no pack for their sales managers and in addition they pay them a percentage of the holdbacks, cash incentives and bonuses from the car manufacturers too.

Lots of these sales managers do not have college degrees and some do not even have high school diplomas, so where the hell else they can get a job that earns them about or over hundred thousand dollars a year with no education? Kissing ass and taking wrong orders from their bosses is what's needed in place of education.

First, they must know how to take orders from their bosses and do everything that they tell them to do without asking questions. Second, they coach salespeople how to mislead and screw customers to make high gross. If sales managers don't have a good gross average they don't have a job in the car dealerships. More gross average means more job security for sales managers, closers and finance managers. Third, take control. Do not let salespeople ask questions about anything, do not let them see the computer and do not let them discuss the reconditioning costs of used vehicles.

Salesmen should be grateful for the opportunity that dealers are giving them to make a living and if they do not like it, the door is open and they can get the hell out.

Fourth, do not be honest with salesmen about their real commissions or pay plans. Most of them do not know how they are getting screwed anyway and like the old saying goes "what they don't know, won't hurt them."

Some of them have their suspicions, they think that they are getting screwed but they do not know how and by whom.

Let them blame parts and service, let them blame the use car manager, let them blame the finance manager, let them even blame you, but we pay you big bucks not to let "the cat out of the bag." Do not let them see invoices, do not let them in the business office to look at files, and most importantly, do not let them know anything. "What they don't know, won't heart them."

Sales managers are members of the sales team too but since their incomes are dependant on the salesmen, fleet, internet and finance manager's productions, they are not included in the term "salespeople."

As crooked and dishonest as most of the car dealers are, they keep coming up with different titles to fool customers and most of all fool their own employees.

I am not trying to confuse, mislead or be negative about the hard work that car salespeople do and I am not trying to put them down or make fun of their titles, I carried those titles for many years too.

My main goal is to open the eyes of commissioned salespeople and show them the reality of what is happening in the car dealerships and help them stop these fucked up, crooked, corrupted and con artist dealers from screwing them anymore.

Every one of these jackass dealers will tell you that they are not doing it but only because they do not have the fucking balls to tell the truth. You can find more shit in their dealerships than in any septic tank.

Greed makes people lie, cheat and be dishonest. Some people want everything for themselves and do not give a shit about others and unfortunately many car dealers are that way.

As far as these crooked assholes are concerned, salespeople can eat hamburgers and tacos everyday and stay in the same one bedroom apartment with their spouse and three kids.

Nothing will change to make the life a little better for the salespeople, it is always going to lean toward the selfish, lazy and asshole car dealer's benefit.

We all know that everybody is in business to make profit but there is a big difference between making profit and ripping people off, especially people that are making you the money. "Do not bite the hands that are feeding you" does not hold true for crooked car dealers.

I have talked to a lot of car salesmen in different car lots and almost all of them are unhappy with what their employers are doing to them.

Selling vehicles is not just a way to kill time for car salesmen/women, it is a day to day living and everyday they hope it gets better but it never does. In reality it is getting worse day after day.

I understand that fleet managers, internet managers and finance managers do not like to be called "salesmen." They have been brainwashed by these con artists that they are managers but if you ask them what or who do you manage? They have no answer. They only manage to make a little paycheck for themselves and a big one for their kinky bosses.

There is one more thing that took me a while to figure out. Why some car dealers do not put the word "salesman" on their retail sales person's business cards? They call them sales representative, sales rep, sales consultant, sales assistant, but not salesman.

These con artists already know that customers do not like salesmen and that is why they put different titles on salesmen business cards in order to mislead their customers.

You are selling their vehicles but to be politically correct, they do not want to label you as a car salesman.

I understand the term sales rep, sales assistant or certified sales bullshit titles, but as far as I know, consultant refers to someone who can give professional advice.

Professions like doctors, lawyers, pharmacists, accountants, engineers and others that require a college degree or some kind of special licensing can be considered consultants.

What kind of consulting can a commissioned car salesperson give to the customers besides trying to make more gross profit out of them per his/her sales managers kinky guidance?

Anyway, no matter what I say, these crooked weasels are way ahead of the game. They already know customers do not like to deal with car salesmen and customers think that they can save some money if they deal directly with a manager, so the dealers came up with the title "fleet Manager."

Some customers think because they are members of some jackass club or credit unions that are milking car dealers to send them referrals, they can get a better deal if they do business with the fleet manager.

These customers do not know that they can get the same deal from the salesmen too if they give them a chance.

They believe that they are getting a better deal from fleet manager just because some internet company or credit union or other jackass club told them to go there and ask for the fleet manager.

What is very unfair and has happened to a lot of retail car sales personnel is this; a sales person may spend a lot of time with a customer and later on sees that customer in the fleet office buying the same vehicle from the fleet manager because he/she was steered by some credit union, internet company or a club.

Unfortunately, most of the time that poor sales person does not get anything for the time that he/she has spent with that stupid and selfish customer. This would just tell you how unfair the auto sales industry is and how disloyal some people are to the car salesmen.

Car dealers also know that almost everyone has a computer and look at their websites, so they figured that they must have a salesman to sell them vehicles as well, but it does not look right to call them internet salesmen. As a result, they came up with another kinky managerial title, the "internet manager."

Knowing that there is a lot of profit to be made by selling warranties, alarms, lo jacks, service plans, gap, interest rates, wax, kill switches and other crap, and also knowing, that changing faces makes a big difference in sales and one sales person can not sell everything by him/herself and even if he/she does, car dealers do not want to pay 20% or 25% commission from the profit of these items to the salesmen, so they came up with the "back end salesman."

Again, since back end salesman does not sound good to the customers, they came up with the title "finance manager" to sell their back end profits by pawning off the crap.

They save a lot of money by not paying a secretary to type contracts or not paying a salesman 20% or 25% commission.

Customers are being turned to trained back end salesmen who schmooze them and sell them what dealers would like him/her to sell and these back end salesmen are called "finance managers."

Secretaries cost money especially if they have to work overtime, but car dealers do not have to pay a dime for the regular time and many occasions for the overtime that their finance managers put in at their dealerships. I ask you a question here?

Can you think of a better way to do business with other peoples money and time without incurring any labor costs?

If you think about this for just a few minutes you will know what kind of crooks we are dealing with here.

These con artists have elevated the slavery to an art. They have found so many ways to get people to work for them without paying them any wages and continuing to boss them around and stealing a good portion of their hard earned money and making them believe that they are blessed to work for them.

Hear me out please, car dealers have very little or in most cases absolutely no investment whatsoever in the items that their finance managers sell. Additionally, they do not pay wages or a salary of any kind to their finance managers but they keep over 85% of the profits for themselves and still look for ways to have their dirty fucking hands in their finance managers pockets to take some of that 15% by putting hidden packs on the accessories.

Some other greedy asshole dealers screw their finance managers more by adding regular packs on the warranties and other items. This is where we see that greed has no limit for these greedy assholes.

These fucking crooks want to keep it all to themselves. They do not give a shit about anyone else.

My fellow salespeople, I know it is hard to move from one car dealer to another, I know it is annoying to listen to the same repeated bullshit that your sales managers and closers are telling you everyday and I know it is embarrassing to answer to your spouse about the $125 paycheck that you took home after two weeks of hard work. I have seen it happening to myself and others but I also know that "everybody wants to go to heaven, but nobody wants to die."

I am not asking you to kill yourselves or die, I want the salespeople to have a better living and enjoy their lives too.

The auto sales industry that we are working for is full of corruption and it is so fucked up that no salesperson can change it by him/herself. They have been using us like salves and have no shame in doing so. These kinky assholes are the firm believer of "why buy the cow when the milk is free?"

How can you change people with that type of mentality? This book will show you how.

Chapter two

SALES DEPARTMENTS

"Over 99 percent of car dealers give the rest a bad name."

Three questions for the salespeople

1 - Are your bosses fair and honest with you about your pay plans?

2 - Do you get any respect from society?

3 - Is selling cars a real job?

IF YOU BELIEVE THAT YOUR CLOSER, sales manager, general manager or the car dealer are being honest about your commissions either you are crazy or you are very new in the car sales industry known as "green pea."

Trusting the puppet closers, sales managers, general managers and specially the con artist car dealers are the biggest mistakes that car salesmen are making. The salesman becomes sheep trusting wolves. They eat you alive and spit you out just like a piece of bone. They walk over you like a cheap carpet and do not give a shit about how hard or how long you have been working for them.

My answer to the second question is based on what I have seen and heard from others. Not only do car salesmen not have a good reputation and are not respected by the society, they do not even get any respect from their own crooked sales managers or the owners of the dealerships that they are working for.

I have seen customers treat the salesmen like they are nobody. They think car salesmen are getting paid to answer their questions and take them on free demo rides. They walk into car lots acting like they are serious buyers and waste the salesmen time for an hour or two without having any real intention of buying. They lie when they walk in and say "we are just looking" and, they lie again when they are leaving telling you "we will be back."

Some of these assholes cannot even buy a hamburger for lunch without getting permission from their spouses. Some cannot finance a $15,000 vehicle if they put down $14,900 and the funny thing is if you ask them are you financing or paying cash? their answer would be "we haven't decided yet."

Some are so upside down that if the salesman asks them are you trading anything? Their answer is no, but after two or three hours of negotiations suddenly a fucking $8,000 negative equity trade in vehicle shows up in the picture.

These jack offs keep going from one car lot to another thinking that a miracle is going to happen that will let them get out of their upside down vehicle without putting any money down. They don't know that miracles do not happen in car dealerships but they keep doing it again and again without informing the salesman about their situation at the beginning.

I blame the dealers for creating jack offs. Dealers do not want to miss a deal so they force their salesmen to tell customers anything that they want to hear on the phone or on the lot to get them inside.

Bad credit? Ok. First time buyer? Ok. Bankruptcy? Ok. Repossession? Ok.

Some of these crooks advertise that "we will pay off your trade no matter how much you owe" but they do not mention anything about that negative equity being added to the price of the new vehicle that is being purchased or in most cases leased.

Anyway, the poor salesman has to go through all kinds of bullshit, demo rides and credit applications that could have been eliminated to begin with. Instead, after few hours of working for nothing, he finds out that the dealer is beating up a dead horse. One, two, or three hours of his time has been wasted for nothing.

Hearing things like; just looking, browsing, killing time or kicking tires are nothing new to the car salesmen.

It has happened to every one of us that after the demo ride in two or three different vehicles you ask them to come inside and make a deal but you hear them saying we are not in the market yet. You want to tell them in their faces that If you are not really in the market to buy, what the fuck are you doing here wasting my time?

Lots of time after a few demo rides you hear other bullshit like; you have been very nice, do you have a business card? Are you working tomorrow? Unfortunately at that point it is a little too late that you found out that they are full of shit and lying to your face. They jacked you off over one hour and now they are leaving and you will never see them again and there is not a damn thing you can do about it unless you believe in the "be back bus" bullshit.

It is frustrating when customers say they have a very good credit but suddenly smoke starts coming out of the credit report machine showing several late charges of 60, 90 and 150 days. They start acting surprised and blame the bank or the post office for their own fuck up.

They said that they are paying cash but after wasting two hours of your time they want to know the best interest rates that banks are offering?

He said that he is a single man when you met him two hours ago but suddenly he wants to talk it over with his fucking wife and when you remind him of saying that he was single he lies to you again and brings out the girl friend or fiancée bullshit.

The point is, salesmen get all of the blame but the real liars are customers and dealers.

Do people think that car salesmans' time is not important and they can waste it as much as they wish? Do they really think that car salesmen have no family to feed or no bills to pay or they think that car dealers are paying their salesmen some salary to put up with their bullshit?

These jack offs are not the real buyers but act like their father owns the fucking dealership. They keep ordering the salesmen to do this and that and the poor salesperson knows that if he/she does not follow their demands and does not take them on demo rides they will get thrown under the bus.

Car dealers do not want to hear any excuses from the salesperson when he lets a customer leaves the lot before that person was turned to another salesman, closer or the sales manager. They do not want to hear that customer does not wear the pants in that family, his wife does even though she is not there with him.

Car dealers do not want to hear that the customer had a repossession two months ago right after his bankruptcy. The salesman has to go through every step of selling and demo-ing the vehicle, get them inside, write them up, get a commitment and take it to the desk. After wasting two hours, the deskman lets him know that customer cannot finance anything. They only qualify for "Chinese" financing and that is known as "one lump sum" which is cash.

I have seen lots of disrespect to the salesmen coming from the sales managers, closers and even general managers. Name calling and discrimination are only very small parts of it. I have seen asshole sales managers that consistently lie to their salesmen, steal money from their front end gross to reduce their commissions or do not give enough money for the customer's trades ins, in order to make themselves look good to the bosses by showing more profit and thus, making the rich richer.

I have seen lots of closers, sales managers and general managers, mother-fucking salesmen, punish them, look down to them or make fun of them in front of others on the show room floor, on the lot and even in the sales meetings which salesmen are forced to attend without getting paid for their time.

I have seen a salesman that had to buy breakfast for the sales team because he was late to work one minute and I have seen a general manager tear up a $1000 finance managers' bonus check in front of the other managers in the managers' meeting because he was twenty seconds late to the meeting just to show that he has the power to do that.

The truth is, when you look at the things that dishonest dealers or their puppet general managers, sales managers and closers are doing to the salespeople, car salespeople are getting more jacked by their bosses than any fucking "lookie loo."

Years ago one of my ex general managers said "screwing sales people is getting to be standard in the auto sales industry."

Car dealers do not give a shit about the salesmen, sales managers and closers do not give a shit about the salesmen and car manufacturers certainly do not give a shit about the salesmen however, they all want the salesmen to sell and make them money.

Car manufacturers have never paid any attention to how salespeople are getting paid or being treated at their franchise car dealerships but they ask dealers to force the salesmen to attend the BDC or any other bullshits like ride and drives or to become certified without paying them anything for their time.

They keep advertising with lines like "come test drive our vehicles" but do not care who is taking these jack offs for the free test drives.

Both car manufacturers and car dealers keep advertising the old "come and test drive our vehicles" line and some car dealers even try to get customers in to their fucking doors by offering cheap gifts like a disposable camera, plastic footballs, five dollar bills, lotto tickets, burger and soda or other bullshit. They offer any type of free farts to bring moochers to their lots to jack their salesmen off.

Just take a look at the ways that car dealers are advertising in the newspapers. They keep putting full page ads while telling their salesmen that they are losing money on the front end gross of the deal in what is called "loss-leader." They claim that these ads cost them few thousand dollars each time.

Do they really lose money in the front end and try to make up their loss in the back end of the deals?

Overall consumers are smarter these days and you do not find as many lay downs as there were before. The days that car dealers were making tons of money on their kinky advertisements like, "slash it sales" which car dealers were jacking up the prices and then slashing it back to where it was or even more than what it was before are over. Now, dealers are advertising left and right with these loss leader bullshit ads and still have hard time to sell their vehicles and even when they sell them with lots of profit in the back end, how much does their hard working salesperson makes? A commission of $50, $75 or $100 called mini

Overall car dealers are ahead of the game by making money from the front end, back end, holdbacks, kick backs, incentives and documentation fees. They also make lots of money from their part and service. Their sales managers get pay a portion of the front and back end profit, cash incentives and hold backs of each new deal. The ones that are getting screwed are the poor salesmen.

Anyway, if the salespeople do not do anything about the abuse, these fucking crooks will keep pissing on us until we die and they feel no shame in doing just that.

Salesmen are not peons but are all too often pissed on. Customers piss on us, sales managers, general managers, dealers and even the closers are pissing on us and let's not forget that car manufacturers are pissing on us too and we are not able to do anything about it.

We are nothing, nobody, zilch, zero, and this will continue unless we help each other and do something about it. For the last several decades these fucking crooks have been pissing on our backs and making us believe that it is raining.

Now, to answer the 3rd question,

If you think selling cars is a job think again and find out what a real job is?

There are big differences between a real job and hope.

A commissioned car salesman goes to work "hoping" that he gets a customer and the buyer financially qualifies to buy. If everything goes the way that it's supposed to, the sales person sells a vehicle and makes a few dollars commission.

We all know that time is money and a real job pays for your time from when you get in to when you get out.

A real job pays extra on the weekends, holidays, overtime and pays for sick days.

A real job pays for meetings, training and trips outside of the company.

A real job will give you enough time to be with your family in the evenings and weekends, and be off on major holidays, but car dealers have changed the weekends and holidays to some kind of "sales event" for their sales team.

Every Friday they brainwash the salespeople in their repeated mandatory and unpaid sales meetings. Even though they set up some weekend bonuses for selling their vehicles, but what they give you compared to what you make for them is a few drop of water from the glass.

Here are some examples of their stupid weekend bonuses:

$5 Cash per write up and $50 Cash per sold unit plus your normal commission.

Some dealers have $100 bonus for selling three units, $200 for four units, $300 for five units. $200 to the sales person for top gross, $200 for top units, $200 for top used and right away they make it sound so big by saying, if you sell four units that include three used vehicles and you have the top gross and top used you already made $800 plus your regular commission.

If you do that every weekend you have another $800 extra just from the bonuses which translates into fifty two weekends a year and makes $41,600 This is an extra income in addition to the commissions that you will be making by selling those units. They do not even consider that you may take off a weekend or two or you may be sick or gone on vacation.

Then they ask those of you, selling four units or more this weekend raise their hands. Everyone including the salesmen that are suppose to be off that weekend will raise their hands because if they don't, they will be questioned as to, why they are not going to work on their weekend off? They will be reminded of how much money they are going to miss by taking off that weekend.

You haven't sold anything yet but, these fucking con artists make it sound like you have already made that $41,600 and if you ask them what about you, Mr. GM? Where are you going to be this weekend? Their reply is "*Nowhere, I am just taking my family to Las Vegas. They haven't been in Vegas since last weekend.*" What about the owner? "*He's been in Hawaii for the last two weeks and loves it so much that he decided to stay another two weeks.*"

Sometimes they trick their salesmen by not giving out any weekend bonuses but they will have huge bonuses for that month and make it sound so big, e.g. $10,000   for   the   top salesman, $7,000 for the second, $5,000 the third, $3,000 the forth and $2,000 the fifth, "If" you sell 500 vehicles this month.

They already know that their average unit sales per month have never been over 250 vehicles but they have no fucking balls to say that there would be no bonuses of any kind for that month. They just jack their salesmen off and 'con' them to work a lot harder for an impossible 'If' for that month.

Anyway, if you busted your ass and put in over forty hours that weekend and sell five units, your commission and bonuses are about $2500 total. God knows how much of that is getting deducted later, but front and back end profit for the dealer including the cash incentives that you do not see, hold backs that you do not see, reserves that you do not see, bonuses that they get from their manufacturers and you do not see, doc fees that no one pays any attention to can be over $15,000 or more and these are not included the normal packs that you know, hidden packs that you do not know and the money that they already hide in the reconditioning costs of their used vehicles and you do not know.

A real job pays for overtime and in some cases double time and you do not get deductions in your paychecks.

How many times have you sold a vehicle and got paid on it but two or three months later you got a deduct on your paycheck and if you questioned it, they say that there was an open R O (repair order) on that deal and how many times you lost half of the commission that you earned because another salesperson wrote that customers' name in the log book?

These bullshit do not exist in a real job. You do not share your money with another salesman who has practically done nothing but a one minute phone pop, log the name and gets half of the commission of your hard work.

A real job pays some profit sharing but these crooked con artists not only avoid paying you any share of their profits, they keep fucking with the commission that they said they pay at your time of employment.

These scumbags screw you when you sell vehicles, screw you when you don't sell and screw you even when you are off. No matter what, you are fucked, with or without vaseline.

A real job wants you to work 40 hours a week with a set opening and closing time. Anything over 40 hours pays overtime and even in some situations double time.

A real job lets you know how many hours you put in and how much money you can expect on your next paycheck. Most of all a real job translates into steady income. Car salesmen never know how much their next paycheck is going to be.

Most of these car dealers give you a time sheet to fill out on paydays instead of a time card that you punch in and out on your shifts. Although you add the hours on the time sheet and most of the time it may be over fifty hours a week (sometimes it can be over seventy hours) dealers don't give a shit. If you haven't made enough commission to make up for it, you will get the minimum wage for the forty hours and as far as they are concerned you can put two hundred hours on the time sheet but if you punch in and out, they must give you time for lunch break and pay you for overtime and etc, but on the time sheet there's no proof of the hours that you have put in unless your sales manager approves it and even so, you will be terminated for not selling enough.

A real job gives you some kind of job security, retirement plan, pension plan, good insurance coverage with dental and vision, vacation pay, sick pay and more importantly pay raise.

You have no "pack" in a real job to take away a chunk of your commission and you do not have to waste the time that you are not getting paid for with, jack offs, in the sales meetings, BDC rooms, unlocking and locking cars, blowing up balloons, ride and drive, being certified and other bullshit that these con artists are coming up with.

Real job gives you pay raises based on the number of the years that you have been with the company but the only raise that car salespeople are getting is "raise in the pack" and that shrinks their paychecks. Car salesmen don't get pay raises, they only get pay cuts.

I can think of few other things that are being offered but very rarely and by very few dealers; Insurance, vacation and 401K are among them. With the ones that do, their insurance are the cheapest one and overall employees pay a big chunk of it from their own pockets.

Their vacation pay is not even enough to buy a round trip plane ticket and most car salesmen can not afford to join in the 401K programs or can not even afford to take a vacation anyway.

In a real job you are respected and your bosses do not invade your privacy and listen to your phone conversations. They do not eavesdrop behind your office doors to see how or to whom you are talking to.

In a real job you have a certain time for lunch break without getting interrupted by some jack offs or your selfish bosses but as a car salesman you must get permission to go grab a hamburger to-go and your selfish sales managers or closers expect you to buy them one too.

Now, let's be honest, we are just slaves who go to these fucking car lots every day and work for practically nothing. We do what they tell us to do and are not paid commensurately. We go to car lots hoping to sell a vehicle and make a few dollars and we call that a job.

A lot of dealers do not even have their pay plans in writing and the ones that do, have no respect for it or do not honor it anyway.

Pay plans mean jack shit to these ass holes. They pay you whatever they want to pay you and whenever they want to pay you and that's the end of it.

If the payday falls on Saturday, every employee will get pay on Friday except the sales team and if payday falls on Friday, the dealer makes all kinds of excuses not to pay the sales team until Monday.

They do not like paydays to fall on Fridays because they do not want the salesmen that are off that weekend to take off. They want every one of their sales personnel to be there and make them money.

You don't know and they don't want you to know that their incomes are depended on you.

Everything is a secret to these con artists. They do not want you to know or see anything. They are the firm believer in; "what you don't know, won't hurt you," and that is not as if they give a shit about your feelings if you find out that they have been screwing you. They keep it secret because they do not want their commissioned sales people keep quitting on them.

We all should have our pay plans in writing and they must honor it. We have to come up with a solution that makes these crooked weasels to take their dirty fucking hands out of our pockets and pay us the correct commissions.

Lets talk about the sales managers and closers now. I have nothing against closers or deskmen, (sales managers) but as soon as they get the managerial position they forget that they were salespeople too.

Their only priority become keeping their crooked boss who gave them the management position happy.

Some of them even bring new ideas of their own to the table on how to screw the salespeople to make themselves look better to their bosses.

As soon as they become closer or a sales manager, they start walking all over the salesmen. They force them to go to more sale meetings and start acting like their father owns the fucking dealership now.

They completely forget who they were and start kissing the bosses ass and sucking their dicks right at the get go.

For your information Mr. closer and sales manager, we all know who gave you the position and who is signing your paychecks, but do not forget that your paychecks are based on the commission too. If salesmen do not sell vehicles and finance managers do not sell anything in the back ends of the deals, you will not have a paycheck. It is as simple as that.

Stop kissing the general managers and owners asses and stop sucking their dicks. If you want to kiss ass, kiss the sales peoples' asses and suck the sales peoples' dicks. They are the ones who are feeding you and making your paychecks. They are the ones who put food on your table and pay your bills. Do not bite the hands that are feeding you even if your greedy bosses ask you to. Have some dignity, have some pride and conscience. Crooks do not trust each other and sooner or later you will be replaced by another asshole. As we all know, nothing is forever. One day you are sales manager or closer and the next day you are back on the line selling or in finance typing. I have seen this happen repeatedly.

As we all know by now, car dealers are not trustworthy. They screw their sales people just like they screw their customers. Sales managers and closers are no exception. If you think that you have a firm grip on your job, think again. Just like the sales people you do not have a job, you only have the opportunity to desk or close deals, do that instead of kissing the owner or the general managers' asses.

After all, you do not have to "go along to get along" with thieves. We all know that there is no honor among thieves. Thieves do not trust anyone and sooner or later another ass kisser will put a knife in your back and throw you under the bus to take your place. Backstabbing is nothing unusual among the managers, closers and salespeople in the car dealerships.

No car dealer or his/her management should be using their power to force their salespeople to do whatever they wish. Control must have a limit, but these crooked con artists have been taking control of their salespeople well above what should be accepted.

Owners and general managers make it clear to their sales managers that to go along, you must get along and its "my way or the highway." These assholes put the nail in the coffin right away and they cut off their sales managers and closers balls as soon as they get the position.

I have been in a lot of the management meetings that car dealers were forcing their managers to attend and I never saw one sales manager having the balls to say something against the bullshit that the general manager or the owner of the dealership were saying. Everyone of them balls were cut off before they got their managerial titles.

By now you should know that I am not trying to teach salesmen how to sell cars and I am not trying to educate customers on how to buy vehicles. All I am trying to tell the sales managers and closers is that you do not have to get along with thieves and you do not have to kiss your boss' ass to keep your job, they need you a lot more than you need them. These assholes are too lazy to work or manage anything themselves. They can only manage to scare the shit out of their general managers in order to make them a complete puppet and that is good enough because their general managers do the same to sales managers and closers and the cycle continues into finance, fleet and salesmen.

These lazy assholes cannot sell a pussy to the troop wagon but they know how to push their general managers into pushing others to make them money, it all come back to the general managers being their puppets.

With the huge amount of money that they pay their general managers they turn them100% in to puppets and force them to regurgitate their influence on others.

One of the first lessons car dealers learn is to keep their salespeople hungry. Never feed them enough and do not let them make too much commission, if you think they are making too much money raise the pack and that will do the dirty job quietly and without creating any heat.

They are aware that "The less you know, the better off they are." They do not want you to know how and how much you are getting screwed at their dealerships and they do not want you to know who the real person is behind all the screwing that goes on at their corrupted dealerships.

They want you to think that the service department is screwing you, they want you to think that parts department is screwing you, they want you to think that finance department is screwing you and they want you to blame the used car manager for the outrageous reconditioning cost of their used vehicles.

These fucking weasels have been putting salespeople together for many years and they want to keep it that way for years to come. They want the salesmen to blame the parts and service departments and the way they have it set up they want the salesmen to blame the finance and used car manager.

That is the way they have been doing business for many years and they have been very successful at it, that is why they keep opening dealership after dealership.

They want you to think others are stealing from you when in fact you don't have to worry about the part, service, used car managers or finance department. The others are these crooked dealers and their puppet general managers who have their dirty greedy hands in your pockets, in the customers' pocket and even in their own manufacturers' franchise pockets.

These crooks screw their franchise factory by making up phony RDR to get the bonuses for unsold vehicles. They lie to their own franchise manufactures by selling non certified used vehicles as the certified ones to get better interest rate and lesser cost for warranty and they cheat banks and financial companies by inflating customers' income on the credit applications to make them qualify for payments that they really can not afford. What makes you think that they will not screw you?

They have been employing cheap labor for so many years that by now it is very hard for them to understand that it is not right. They have been cheating customers and screwing their employees for so many years that they do not even know how to do business fairly.

Every morning that they wake up, they take a Viagra. They do not take Viagra to have sex with their wives or fuck their mistresses or girl friends. They take it to fuck with peoples pockets and it has gone to their fucking brains and blood by now.

They do not care if these people are customers or employees. They want every ones money. They want to have their dirty fucking hands in every ones pocket. They think of every possible way to get people to work for them with the minimum amount of money needed to be paid for labor and they try very hard to pay the least commission without letting the salespeople see the real cost and the real profit and that has been working very well for them.

They pay you what they want to pay you not what you really earned.

They always use slaves and the sad part is that these slaves do not even have the right to ask questions. Dealers mentality runs along the lines of "what you see is, what you get."

They hold your $700 commission on a deal for another two weeks because the customer gave them $200 post dated check.

The finance manager got paid on that deal as did the sales manager and general sales manager and the general manager. Why didn't the salesman? He is the creator of the deal and he is the one who needs the money most. It is called "control."

They control you any way they can and if you ask questions, you are bad apple, you are an OBT, you are whiner, you are being negative and you are poison.

A lot of big companies in America send their materials to India, Pakistan, Mexico, Korea or China because labor is cheap in those countries. Car dealers have been using cheap labors here in America and have been getting away with it for many years all in the name of "commission."

As an employer, they have the right to set your schedule and tell you when you come to work and when to leave even if your shift is over or it is after the closing time. They can still make you stay without paying you any money.

They are not paying for your time but they tell you when to come to the dealership and when to leave.

As a sales person I have worked many days that I was supposed to be off. I have worked many weekends though I was to be off and I have worked many holidays that I was not scheduled to work.

I have worked many unexpected hours on my off days or off shifts for stupid meetings, ride and drive or appointments that customers did not show up to or even if they did, we could not make the deal.

I have heard all kind of lies and bullshit from customers and I have seen thousands of strokes and jack offs on car lots in my life and finally I came up with this conclusion:

The biggest jack offs in the auto sales industry are, the crooked car dealers, their cock sucking general managers, ass kissing sales managers and weasel closers. They are so full of shit that they even put the septic tanks to shame.

It is unfortunate that salespeople have known about these for many years but they have not done anything to stop it.

Some have had the balls to tell these crooks to take your fucking hands out of our pockets. They got fired and went to another dealership and started working there. Soon they found out that these assholes are all the same shit in different toilets.

Seeing the same shit at different lots makes the salespeople puke but what can they do? If they open their mouths, they will get fired again. Their only other option is If they want to be car salespersons in the car dealerships let these fucking thieves keep stealing from them.

I said it at the beginning of this book, these greedy assholes do not give a shit about people, rules, laws or regulations. They are crooks and thieves with the money and have been getting away with their un lawful business practices since Henry Ford created the Model T.

They have been dishonest for so many years that by now it will take a lot to change their fucked up way of thinking.

Chapter three

FINANCE MANAGERS

"Over 99 percent of car dealers give the rest a bad name."

I NEVER DREAMED THAT ONE DAY I would be a car salesman but life took me in that direction and I started selling vehicles as a green pea salesman in Southern California.

Just like other salesmen I stayed out side of the building saying "coming in, coming in, coming in" until I finally got an up (customer). I showed them a few cars and piqued their interest in one, took them on a demo ride and wrote them up and got some kind of commitment and turned them over to my closer and more than half an hour later I was told to put the vehicle in the wash rack and take your customer to the finance office.

After months of selling vehicles in the T - O stores, I gained enough experience to close my own deals and started looking for a straight sales store and got the opportunity to sell vehicles at a franchise dealership.

I always wanted to get experience in the finance department and learn about the back end gross profit that car dealers were making.

Customers and even lots of salesmen, do not know anything about the millions of dollars profit that car, motorcycle, boat and RV dealers are making in the back end of the deals at their dealerships every year.

After more than four years working on the line at the same dealership I pushed and pushed until they put me in the finance.

After a month or two working in the finance department I started to realize why car dealers call their back end salesmen finance managers. I could see then what kind of con artists I have been working for over the last few years as a salesman and I found out later that this was not the only dealership that was screwing their own sales people, majority of them were doing it as well.

By using the word "majority" I mean a lot more than fifty percent.

Car dealers are not Mother Theresa and they are not there to do you a favor as an employer if you are their employees or help you save some money if you are one of their customers. The only person that they care or give a shit about is "themselves."

After years of experience I found out that dishonest car dealers are the most selfish, spoiled, lazy, single minded and greedy assholes out there. I do not give a shit who they are, how many dealership they own or how much dirty money they have.

Most of them are a bunch of fucking crooks and should be in prison behind bars instead of screwing people left and right in their dealerships.

Crooked car dealerships are built on foundations of dishonesty and stand on four simple letters across four different segments of their dealerships. The four simple letters are "f u c k" and the four departments are, "sales, finance, service and parts."

They train and coach their salesmen to fuck the customers in their sales departments by payment packing and a tool called "four square" to high gross them during purchase or by doing their best to switch them to their rip off lease programs to even make more front or back end gross profit.

Their finance managers in the finance department are trained to schmooze and then fuck the customers and make huge back end gross profit for them.

Their service advisors are known to fuck the customers and sell them a lot of unnecessary repairs and finally they fuck customers in their part departments because almost every item that is being sold in the dealerships' parts departments can be found a lot cheaper elsewhere.

What is amazing about the way these four departments are set up is that each one is making profit from the others as well as the customers but overall, most of the profit goes to the owners' pocket without him/her even being anywhere near the dealership.

Not working gives them more than enough time to think of different tricks to screw others and one of these tricks is to let the service, part and finance departments make profits from the sales department and since the percentage of commission is a lot less in the other three departments than the sales department, dealers make a lot more money that way and they do not give a shit if their sales team is getting screwed.

The parts department sells to service and then the service department screws sales and finance managers by charging more than retail cost on the parts and labor. Finance department screws salesmen and sales managers steal from the front end gross of the salesmen and put it in the back end. The bottom line is, every department at the dealership screws the poor salesmen.

I do not think that I was perfectly clear in describing the personalities of dishonest car dealers on the page 42 of this book. In addition to selfish, spoiled, lazy, single minded, greedy and assholes, I would like to add, ignorant, arrogant, corrupted and extremely controlling sons of the bitches.

They live on the big money that their employees are making for them and they think that their shit do not stink and their farts do not smell. They are above every thing including the law because they have the money to pay their lawyers to find the smallest of technicalities in the law and protect their asses in courts or arbitrations.

They pay tens of thousands of dollars each month into the hands of their general managers to run their places and screw the customers in their sales, finance, part and service departments. They also cheat the government by a lot of phony tax write offs and hiding the real profits that they are supposed to pay taxes on and most of all they screw their own salespeople out of their real fair share of commissions in a lot of different ways.

Before I go any further I want to ask you a simple question. Have you ever had a feeling that something is not right but you can't pinpoint it? It is like you're unable to prove it and more importantly you are not allowed to see or question it.

You know that you just got screwed or in the process of getting screwed but you have no way of proving it and you have no idea how and by whom you are getting screwed? You feel it, you smell it and you even taste it but because you do not see it, you cannot prove it. They just do not let you investigate or question it.

Most of the times that I sold a new vehicle especially if it was leased, and I really can say that almost every time that I sold a used vehicle I knew there should have been more front end gross profit.

I knew that my commission should have been a lot more than what the car dealer said it was but as a salesman I had no right to see any of the documents or ask questions about my commissions. I just had to accept what ever they were telling me.

I knew that I was getting screwed but I was unable to prove it. I just had to believe those ass kisser dishonest deskmen even though they didn't have the fucking balls to stand up to their bosses and say stop making us steal from these poor salesmen and put it in your fat pockets.

As a car salesman I was not allowed to look at the dealer's computer or look at the invoices and look at any reconditioning cost of the used vehicles that I was selling. I was not allowed in the business office nor was I even allowed to question my sales managers about my commissions on any deal that I made.

All I heard after selling a vehicle was a "good job" bullshit. Those crooked sales managers would not even tell me how much my real front end gross profit was.

Knowing their own crooked bosses, they had to manipulate everything to their benefit. What they told me when I sold a vehicle was never taken into the account later. It was as though they never said it any way.

The reality was, after a few months of selling vehicles I could not count on the commission voucher that I received that day or any other day. Those vouchers did not mean anything, they never increased though most of the time they were getting reduced.

God knows how many times my $400 or $600 commission vouchers changed to a $50 or $100 mini and a few times they even ended up as nothing because the vehicle was unwind.

I worked hard when I sold it and now I have to go get the miles of the odometer, pick up the RS from the windshield, give it to the finance manager and park the unwind vehicle in the bone yard, all of the work for nothing.

Some of my pay from the last few paychecks was deducted on the deals that I had sold three or four months ago for some unknown reason. I had no choice but to accept it and that happened quite often.

One of the first things a car salesman learns is, "deduct commission vouchers." You get mad, you get pissed and you use the "F" word, but all you can do is complain or bitch about it.

We all know how unfair it is to work for nothing but they make you believe it is a part of the car business.

Every salesman knows about deduct commission and unwinds. We all have done work for nothing or mini commissions.

I think that if I had added up all of the deduct commission vouchers and unwinds I could have had several thousand dollars more in my bank account but as we all know salesmen have no say in anything but to accept what they are paying us.

I started digging into the deals that I sold or leased myself before. Whether the transaction happened over the last few months or years I found out a lot of things that I never knew before even though I worked as a salesman in the same corrupted toilet over four years.

They gave me a limited password to work with their computer and they wanted me to sell whatever garbage that would make profit for the dealer by improving back end gross profits of the deals. This would only help to make more money for the car dealer. More money for dealer meant more commission for sales managers, general sales manager and the general manager because they all were on commission too but with different pay plans and profit percentages.

Just like any other finance managers, I was on 100% commission too. There was no guaranteed salary or promises of any kind. I was only told to push, push and push to sell. Do not take 'no' for an answer, ask and ask, push and push again until customer caves and buys whatever that fucking car dealer had me sell.

"What is your average back end gross profit?" they would ask? Their expectation was at least $1000 average gross profit per vehicle from each one of their back end salesmen (finance managers.)

Finance managers were not permitted to give any excuses either. Again, there were to be no "ifs, ands or buts" of any kind.

The number of cash deals, short term leases or number of customers from India, Pakistan, Iran, Arab countries and especially people from Asia, who are known as hard negotiators and are not laying down for car dealers bullshit programs or fall in to their traps did not make any difference to the car dealers. No good back end average gross profit means no job security.

Usually when a finance manager picks up a deal from the rack that is ready to be typed, the first thing that he/she wants to know is If that customer is financing, paying cash or wants to get the option contract to go to his/her own bank or credit union?

The second is what the customers name and nationality is and the third is what do they do for living?

If the deal is cash or option contract or customers name is from some specific foreign country, it automatically put an "F" word in their mouth and they make a long face and start having a very negative attitude toward the salesman who is selling that unit.

As far as customers nationality goes, lots of finance managers don't even try to sell anything. They get frustrated and just want to type that deal fast and hope to make up their lost time on the next customer.

An experienced car salesman will drop the up (customer) that he called right a way, when he notices that customer is Asian, Middle Eastern or from India Afghanistan or Pakistan. It is not out of prejudice, it is only because, he knows that it would take at least three hours of negotiation to make a mini deal and yet later on get a bad CSI.

I have seen Asian salesmen refuse to take care of their own homeboys and salesmen from Middle East do not get excited about selling vehicles to their countrymen. That is not because they do not like each other. It is because they know each other better and also know it is not worth their time.

Unfortunately when you are finance manager and have to type deals for, Nguyen, Chang, Chen, Gao, Singh, Patel, Awad, Deeb, Tran, Ahmed, Akhtar or some fucking Hajji Baba from Iran, not only you do not sell anything and fail to make any money, your average back end gross will drop down too.

As a result, there is a big chance that you will lose your little bonus too. It will be a double whammy but your sales managers, general manager and specially the dealer do not want to hear it.

They pretend that you must be honest with customers and close them smooth by selling them garbage in the back, but they know deep in their hearts that you must be a liar, cheater and a crook in order to confuse the hell out of the customers by payment packing or scare the shit out of them in different ways to sell them your crap to have high back end gross average.

Car dealers are the most disloyal employers out there. There is a well known saying "what have you done for me lately?" They do not care about last month or two or three months ago, they don't care about last year, they want to know, what you are doing for them now?

They are not paying you any wages or salary, but they always want you to make them money because their incomes are depending on your performances and it does not make any difference to them if you are a finance manager selling the crap in the back or you are a salesman selling vehicles on the line, in fleet or on the internet.

They act like you need them but the real truth is, they need you a lot more than you think.

You feed them, they are not feeding you. You are the one who stays outside in 100 degree heat or freezing cold trying to get an "up"

We all know "time is money" and it is your time that these schmucks are using to their benefit without paying you a dime. Time is money and they are stealing your money everyday, whether it is the weekdays, late at nights, weekends or holidays. You are working and making them money while they are sleeping or having good times with their family and friends.

If you go home blank, not only do they do not give a shit, they may even give you dirty looks and even question you.

They do not care if you did not make any money for yourself, they are unhappy because you did not make any money for them.

Most of the time there is a very good chance that for every one dollar that a salesman makes the dealer makes ten, twenty or even fifty times more.

Almost every time you sell or lease a vehicle to customers that are upside down on their trades, you make a mini voucher but the dealer makes several thousand dollars in the back end and that is not including the hold backs that manufacturers pay them and you do not know how much it is and even if you find out you don't get a penny of it any way.

As a car salesmen we all have gone blank for a few days or even a couple of weeks but your closer, any sales manager, general manager or the owner would never say, take this $100, I know you have not sold a vehicle lately and you need to put some food on the table for your family, Instead, they give you dirty looks, insult you and make you feel guilty.

They may even joke about you and say things like "fucking guy hasn't sold a car in a week and has the balls to ask to leave ten minutes early tonight!"

They do not want you to know that their income is dependent on you but that is the truth and the truth hurts, especially when you are working for some crooked, con artist and scumbag dealers and their ass kissing management team.

You may think that I must have something against closers, sales managers or general managers. I really don't. I just do not have respect for the ass kissers that do not care if others are getting screwed as long as they are getting paid good money to cover up for their crooked, selfish and lazy bosses.

In fact I have lots of respect for the honest car guys however, in my life being a car salesman, fleet, internet and finance manager, I saw one honest general manager, few honest sales managers and one honest used car manager all working at the same car dealership.

I did not know the owner that well but he must have been an honest man because a lot of kinky and unfair things that I have seen happening to the salespeople at other car dealerships was not happening to the salespeople in his dealership. They had pack for their retail salesmen but I knew that they were not stealing from them.

The truth is, every sales manager and closer knows if his salespeople are getting screwed by the dealer or his puppet general manager by using unfair packs or inflating the cost of reconditioning used vehicles but most of them keep their mouth shut and do not say anything.

They become one of the boys and keep moving money around to the owners benefit by stealing from the front end gross and hiding it in the back end, or the way that they were told to appraise the trade ins.

An ass kissing sales manager is the one who knows members of his sales team are getting screwed by the owner or his general manager but instead of doing some thing about it, he will bring some of his own ideas to the table to make it easier for those scumbags to screw the poor salespeople more.

They do not care who is getting screwed and work just like prostitutes, brown nosing, kissing asses and sucking dicks, and we all know the end of the line for each whore, unfortunately there is no happy ending.

Just take a look at the way sales people' schedules are made:

One day you work in the morning one day you work in the evening, one day you work bell to bell and one day you are off. The next week you have the opposite schedule. Where you once worked in the morning you are now working on the evening shift. It is all mixed up.

Reason for it is they do not want you to have another job, part time or full time. That is called "control."

If a car salesperson sells a vehicle at one o'clock in the morning and finance manager has to stay and type the deal at that late hour, there are no extra commission or any bonuses for them of any kind.

Take a good look at your pay plans and that is 'if' they gave you a copy to keep.

There is something there called the "pack" and they can raise it anytime to shrink your income and that is "control."

It means they can control your paychecks and the more years you have been working for the same asshole, the more he has been cutting your income off.

The same rules apply for the finance managers too. Their hours are mixed up and a lot of dealers have hidden packs on most of the items that their finance managers sell as well.

There are some greedier dealers out there that even have regular pack on the warranty, auto care and other bullshit. Their finance managers know it but again, they can not say or do anything about it.

Dealers do it to control their F&I peoples' income and if a finance manager says something or complains about it, he/she will lose their opportunity to sell.

When you get a job at a dealership, they call you "employee at will" and that means they can fire you anytime. You have no employment contract with them, all you have is a changeable pay plan and they can change it anytime they want. If you do not like the changes, the door is open and you can leave.

You are employed at will, you have no right to say anything against what they are doing.

Now, lets go back to the time that I was finance manager and how I found out about the tricks that dealers are using to screw their salespeople.

The limited computer password I had allowed me to look at the deals structure and figure out how the money was being moved around to the car dealers benefit. I realized how the money kept going to the same fucking pocket called the dealer's pocket.

I would like to explain what moving money around is, so when I say car dealers keep moving the money around to their best benefit you can understand it better.

Car dealers train their deskmen (sales managers) and finance managers to move the money around on the deals to work to their best benefit all the time.

Just suppose the salespersons are on the 25% commission after the pack and the finance managers getting an average of 10% commission from the hard and soft ads and the reserve. This is how car dealers keep getting ahead by moving the money around to their own benefit:

If the front end gross after the pack was $3000, the 25% commission for the salesman would have been $750. Since the salesman can not see the invoice or the cost, sales manager can steel $1000 of the front end and puts it in the back end. Salesmans' commission would decrease to $500. Poor salesman loses $250 in real money. Finance manager gets 10% of that $1000 and he is happy making free $100 by selling nothing so he keeps his mouth shut, sales manager makes his commission from that $1000 and the crooked dealer keeps the rest which is close to $150.

It is not just one --- one $150. It is a lot more when you adding them up in one month and one year. There is an old saying "oceans are made by drops of water."

One $150 here, another $300 there, $3000 phony recon, $600 Pack, $200 alarm, $300 warranty, $450 from the non certified used vehicle and they add up from different deals and suddenly becomes about $80,000 to over $100,000 a month and close to or over one million dollar a year that crooked dealer was not paying commissions on to his/her salespeople.

25% of that money is close to or over $250,000 real money that the dealer was stealing from his/her sales team a year.

I do not know the tricks that they use to screw their employees in service and part departments but as far as I know, if they are not honest with their salespeople, they are not honest with other employees either.

Another example of moving money around is called "payment packing."

Payment packing is a very old trick that was designed by dealers to confuse the consumers who finance or lease their vehicles and steer their concentration from the price on to the monthly payments.

Some car buyers do not care how long the term of the loan or lease is, or how much they are paying for the vehicle in the long run. They do not consider the interest that they are paying or how much that warranty, paint protection or alarm is really costing them.

A dealer can sell them a three year warranty for whatever price the bank would advance for it and customers would not care as long as the car payments are within their budget.

Dealers love customers that finance or lease their vehicles with them and since they are closed on the payments, dealers take the maximum advantage by screwing them on the price and interest rate as well as other profitable crap that their finance managers sell in the back end of the deals.

I told you before about the loss leaders advertisements that car dealers put in the newspapers on the weekends. They pay lots of money for their ads every weekends knowing that more than 85% of customers finance or lease their vehicles and they have a very good chance of recovering the little money that is lost on the front end of loss leaders ads.

Overall, dealers will come ahead by several thousand dollars at the end of the weekends.

Dealers do not care about the cash buyers that much and perpetually hope that every customer finance or lease their vehicle so they can payment pack the shit out of them and make tons of money on the front and back end of each deal.

The reality is, most of the profit that car, RV, boat or motorcycle dealers are making in front and back end of the deals come from the payment buyers and car dealers consistently train their salespeople to switch the cash buyers to payment or even better, switch them to the lease.

Now, let's see how payment packing works? After a few rounds of dickering between the salesman, sales manager and customer, the sales manager pencils on the work sheet in big numbers (ok you win.) Only $750 down and $387 a month.

The customer agrees on the payments and since he is a payment buyer and can afford $387 a month car payment he is happy with the deal and ready to walk into the finance office, sign the papers and drive home with his new or previously owned vehicle.

Deskman and finance manager both know that the customers real payments based on his credit rating are $355 a month, but the customer doesn't know that. The sales manager has left a big leg for the finance manager and it is the finance managers job to bump this customer up a few more dollars and move the money around to improve the deal and make the most profit from this leg for the dealer, and since sales managers and finance managers are both on commission, the more profit in the back end to the dealer means more commission to both of them too.

At this point the finance manager already has $32 leg and if he bumps this customer 50 cents more a day ($15 dollars a month) plus the $32 dollars leg that he has already, he's got a total of $47 per month. He had enough time to calculate all of the numbers already and when customer gets to the finance office, he/she offers the customer a nice bullshit package of warranty, alarm and paint protection with which the finance manager can make a big back end profit for the house and a good commission for him or herself too.

If the customer is closed on 60 months there are $47 x 60 months = $2820. The maximum cost for these three items on a four cylinder car to the dealer is not more than $1200 and the dealer is ahead over $1600 profit in the back end (That is not including the hidden packs) and the finance manager gets to keep about 10% of that which is $160 as his commission.

Unfortunately most of the time, payment buyers end up paying a lot more on the same vehicle than cash buyers and if they leased the vehicle, they will be paying even more.

Sometimes you hear a customer saying that the finance manager was such a nice person. He/she gave us a warranty, alarm and paint protection for only $15 more a month.

These customers do not know 2 + 2 is 4. They do not even use their common sense to get a pencil and calculator to see $15 x 60 months is $900. How can $900 buy $1995 warranty, $695 alarm and $130 protection for the car paint? They don't even see the cost for alarm or paint protection on the contract. It was all added together with the selling price. (California law has been changed now and dealers must disclose the term and the price of every item.)

The numbers just do not jive but these customers are so dumb that they cannot calculate a simple mat.

Some even say that the finance manager was such a nice person and gave us a free alarm.

These customers do not know that nothing is free and the finance manager is not in love with them and would not even kick them in the ass for free.

Anyway, I started looking at my own previous deals when I was a salesman at the same place and the more I looked, the more I found out how bad I was getting screwed when I was working there on the line.

I started to dig a little more. I thought maybe they were only screwing me but when I looked at the other salesmen's deals, I saw, oh boy, it was not just me that was getting screwed, they had done it to every salesman and they are still doing it to them left and right.

Did I say screw? Sorry, screw is too much of an understatement word for what that con artist dealer, his crooked general manager and his kinky sales managers were doing to the sales people. We were getting fucked left and right by those assholes.

Like I said, being a finance manager is only a title. It is just another way for these con artists to fool their back end salesmen and make them believe that they are now managers too. They are lead to believe that they are one of the boys and as a result they do not let the dealers secrets out.

I was carrying a manager title. I was finance manager but I had no clue what the fuck or who the hell I was managing?

I did not even have the authority to unwind a deal that was turned down by every bank or financial institution. I had to go to the sales manager or finance director and then they both had to go to the general manager to get an ok to unwind that deal.

The harsh reality was that I was not managing jack shit. I was only typing deals and selling the garbage that they wanted me to sell inside that little office.

I really was the same salesman with a managers title and I was the same free horse only with a different saddle.

I was on 100% commission and no salary. I wasn't guaranteed anything except a lot more hours. I had to stay until the last customer leave and only after the salesman delivered the sold unit to the last customer could I leave.

By talking to other finance managers who had more experience in the finance department I learned that my real job was to scare the shit out of customers to sell them something and improve the back end gross to make my own commission.

The more I sold and the higher prices that I sold the garbage for the more I made for the company and since I was on 100% commission, the more profit I made for the dealer the more I made for the general manager and every sales manager and myself.

At the finance department our real job besides typing deals and doing legal paper work for banks and the DMV that we were not getting paid for was to sell, sell, and sell.

I was one of the boys now, I had a limited password to their computer and learned how to move the money around for the dealer's benefit. I was able to see in the computer what was happening before and what is happening now and how they have been screwing their salesmen before and how they are doing it to them now.

I have sold thousands of cars for many years and have a lot of respect for each and every hard working car salesman/women, their job is not easy and nobody appreciates what they do.

They get no respect from customers, they do not have a good reputation in the society and they do not even get any respect from their own employers.

Customers that they sold a vehicle to, are not their customers, they are the dealers customers until there is a heat, or something goes wrong and then they suddenly become the salespeople's customers.

They do not get pay for their time let alone overtime, weekends or holidays. They do not have a good health insurance policy with vision and dental for the most part and they do not have sick pay, pension or any kind of retirement plan. Some do not even get any vacation pay.

Car salesmen make their living only if they sell a vehicle but car dealers force them to do a lot of other things without paying them anything for doing it.

Some car dealers have a 401 K plan, but with the paychecks

that the average car salesman is making, lots of them are not able to participate in it.

Most of car dealers would not hire any employee if he/she does not agree with their arbitration clause which is on the last page of their employment applications and it is the only place that a new employee can sign that application.

Arbitration takes away the right of any employee to go to trial by the jury in case something happens later on during their employment, whether they get hurt on the job or find out that their employers have been screwing them on their pay plans.

Car salespeople must accept any pay cut which is imposed upon them by the car dealers raising the pack. They must go to all kinds of bullshit meetings without getting paid for their time even on their days off.

These con artists make their meetings mandatory for their salespeople and not only do they not pay for their time, they are too fucking cheap to pay for their gas or even buy them a cup of coffee.

In fact they arrange it so that salesmen go to some bullshit ride and drive or other manufacturer training inside or outside of the dealerships on their off shift or off days so their fucking floors be covered by on duty salesmen.

Salesmen have no say so of any kind toward these schmucks for flooding their floors. The number of salespeople on their shift keeps rising and salespeople cannot say anything about the open floor policy that these crooks are pulling on them.

Let me explain the advantage of having the open floor policy for the car dealers to the new salesmen.

By now you should know that car dealers do not give a shit about anyone or anything unless there is a benefit in it for them. Things like "customer satisfaction" known as CSI does not mean jack shit to these crooks. They only follow that because their franchise headquarter is forcing them to be nice to the customers otherwise as far as they are concerned: "fuck everybody."

They make their living by sucking the blood out of everyone

including their own employees. They never let their conscience take over their business decisions no matter who the customer or employee is.

These cheap bastards put a penny between their asses and squeeze it hard to get the copper out. That is how cheap and kinky they are.

I told you before, foundation of their businesses are built on the 'fuck' and if you think they give a fuck about you as an employee or as a customer you are fucked already but you do not know it yet.

The number of car salesmen does not make any difference to car dealers because they are on commission but it makes a big difference to the salespeople incomes. More salesmen mean more competition and more hard work for the individual resulting in less of a chance to get an up or phone pops. The same goes for fleet, internet, and even finance managers (Except phone pops for finance managers).

A lot of salesmen quit if the dealer hires too many salesmen but these con artists have it down to an art.

Instead of hiring extra salesmen, they leave their floors open at any time so their regular salesmen can work on other shifts too, and since car dealers keep their salesmen hungry, there is a very good chance that a few salesmen will be working on other shifts besides their own.

You may not believe this, but I once saw a salesman at a car dealership with the open floor policy worked one whole month from the opening time in the morning until closing time at night without taking a day off. I honestly can say he put in an average of eighty or more hours in that dealership over the course of each week that month and the management did not object to that at all.

There is no way a dealer lets a porter, cashier or an office employee who is on the time clock put even fifty hours in one week because of the overtime that they must pay but since salesmen are making commission, dealers do not give a shit and in fact they want every one of their salesmen to put more hours in and above his or her schedule.

Dealers do not have a set time for the sales peoples lunch and not a real set closing time for their sales departments. As long as there is a lookie loo on the lot, there must be one or more salesperson to cover the lot even if it is way past the closing time.

Car dealers have been screwing their sales people left and right for so many years and in so many different ways that it's difficult to imagine the infinite variations.

Every one of these crooks can write a book about "how to screw the commissioned employees" better than the other one.

As long as they make their money and keep adding zeros to their bank accounts, they do not care who is getting fucked, customers or employees.

When I talk about car dealers, I mean the owner or owners of the dealerships and their puppet general managers who have no choice but to follow their bosses guidelines to save their own very well paid jobs. Also I am talking about some ass kisser closers and sales managers that knowingly follow the unfair business practices of their bosses.

I have already told you, there is no honor among thieves. Thieves do not trust anyone because they are always afraid that they may get caught and for that reason dealers do not want their salesmen to see or know what they are doing. Car dealers do not allow their salesmen in the business office not because they are afraid that the salesmen may screw the girls that are working there, they are not allowed because dealers are afraid that salesmen may look at files and figure out how they are getting screwed.

Salesmen are not allowed to see any of the invoices for new vehicles nor do they have permission to question reconditioning costs of used vehicles. Sales managers are afraid that salespeople would find out how their bosses are packing invoices on new and inflating reconditioning cost on the used vehicles to screw them out of their fair share of commissions.

If the owner is a fair and honest person and wants to make his money in an honest way but the ass kissing general manager is kinky and dishonest, then it would not take the owner any time to find out what is going on and get rid of the kinky son of the bitch. However, most of the time greed takes over the owners conscience and he acts like he doesn't know where the hell his profit is coming from. That makes him guiltier than the one who runs his corrupted business.

You may ask why have I stayed in the car business for so many years if I did not trust the car dealers from the start?

I got into the car business in my late thirties. I did well as far as selling and I made a decent living the years that I was working in fleet and finance. One paycheck was good, one was bad and one was really bad, but just like other salespeople, I made a paycheck to paycheck living.

I do not hate every car dealer, I only hate the dishonest ones. The ones that their mentality revolves around "give me, give me and give me a lot more." Unfortunately they out number the honest ones by a lot, and I mean, a lot, a lot, a lot.

It did not make any difference which car dealer I was working for, all except one. They were all the same charlatan, crook and con artist with different names, different brand name and different addresses.

They all called themselves "number one" of some kind of bullshit. One was number one volume dealer in the county, one was number one in service and one was number one in customer satisfaction. One was just putting a big "one" on the billboard without even mentioning what the fuck he is number one for? All I know is, majority of them are number one in screwing customers and employees.

These assholes have no mercy for anybody. You can be their cousin, you can be their neighbor, you can be their high school friends, you can be the police chief, county sheriff, district attorney, FBI agent or even work for the DMV, it doesn't matter, they still try to screw you. They may go a little easy on you in their sales and finance departments but they catch up with you sooner or later in their part and service departments.

In dishonest car dealerships, the kinkier you are and higher front end gross you make for them, the better chance you have to get in the management position and the same goes for the finance managers too.

The more back end gross that you can make for the dealer, the better chance for you to become sales manager or finance director.

To them you are strong because you are good at screwing people.

As a non commission employee you have the choice of changing jobs or working for another company but as a commissioned car salesman since most of these assholes are crooks, if you quit your job at one dealer and start fresh in another one you know that the same shit is going to happen to you again.

In other words, unless you hit the jackpot and find an honest dealer, the sky is the same color in almost all of them unless you get out of this corrupted business and get in a different type of job, a real job.

It may be the nature of car business that uneducated management systems are so fucked up that general managers has to keep kissing the owners' asses, sales managers keep kissing the general managers' asses and closers keep kissing sales managers' asses.

Unfortunately I have to admit that there are a lot of ass kisser salespeople out there too that are looking for opportunities to get promoted or get spooned.

The funny thing is that car dealers teach their salespeople if, "customers' lips are moving, they are lying" when in fact, these crooked con artist are the biggest liars themselves.

Anyway, not paying the minimum wage leaves the car dealers' greedy hands open to hire as many salespeople as they want. This is called "flooding the floor" and as a salesperson we have all seen it but there was nothing that we could do about it.

A dealer may sell hundred vehicles a month with ten salesmen or they could do the same with fifteen salesmen. They could have one fleet or internet manager or three, two finance managers or four. It doesn't matter, more members on the sales team will not hurt car dealers financially that much however, it does impact the salespeople a lot.

If car dealers had to pay commission plus the minimum wages to the salespeople, a lot of bullshit like being at the dealership at eight in the morning, being in the BDC or follow up room, flooding the floor, open floor policy, unnecessary daily meetings, or mandatory weekly meetings would never happen.

Sending salespeople to ride and drives whether they are on shift, off the shift or on their off days to learn about the new vehicles that manufacturers are coming up with would stop right away and their sales department would not be open at eight in the morning with six salesmen doing nothing but bullshitting with each other.

They would not keep six salesmen, a closer, and two finance managers late at night just in case a lookie loo shows up.

No salesman had to be in the service area at 7 o'clock in the morning to see if a service customer wants to trade his/her old vehicle because it is not worth to repair but these kinky slave drivers keep their sales people to the last minute even if it is late at night and raining like hell.

Most of them send their receptionist home at 6 pm when their parts and service department close because they are too cheap to pay few dollars per hour to some one to answer their phone after 6 pm, sales team must do that after the receptionist is gone.

I have worked for car dealers that did not have a porter after 6 pm, but their sales departments were open until ten at night and poor salesmen had to wash the vehicles that they were selling after six o'clock or had the customer bring them back the next day to get washed.

Overall, these selfish, lazy assholes are making life a lot harder for their sales people and a lot easier for themselves.

As a commissioned car salesman you have to depend on yourself 100% of the time to support you and your family. You have to cover the lot and at the same time, listen to the sales pages to answer the sales calls. You always have to watch your back to make sure that you are not getting skated by other salesmen.

Most of the time you stay outside rain or shine, hot or cold, days, evenings or nights, weekends and holidays keep saying "coming in, coming in, coming in" until you get an up.

This up (customer) is a complete stranger that you do not know anything about and have never met before. You have to do your walk around on a few vehicles and take them on number of test drives until you land them on the vehicle that they like. Next, you start filling out the credit app, run the credit and pull out the work sheet to negotiate the price and payments. Going back and forth between the sales manager and the customer for one or two hours until you close the deal, shake hands and put the vehicle in wash rack to be washed.

As usual the fucking porter is not there and you have to page the minimum wage employee who barely speaks English two or three times to get his ass to the wash rack and wash the sold unit. Fill up the tank if the vehicle is new or certified, have extra keys ready, find the owners manual package, delivery sheet handy and after the customer comes out of the finance, stick the RS on the window, explain the fixtures and switches in the vehicle, thank them for their business and wait till they hit the curb.

You hear a "good job" bullshit from the sales manager and that is almost the end of that picture for now.

A day or two later you call that customer and thank them again and want to make sure that they are happy with their car and your service.

You ask for referrals to see if their family members, friends, neighbors or even their fucking dogs or cats are in the market to buy a vehicle and more importantly you beg them "please, please, please," when you get the survey, make sure that you check mark that you are "completely satisfied" so, our ass hole owner can get his presidential award from the manufactures' headquarter to shove it in his big lazy fucking ass, as that would make it easier for him to open his next dealership to screw more customers and employees.

You have done everything from the start to finish with a little help from the deskman who all this time was sitting on his ass behind the desk and punching a couple of numbers on the computer. All he did was write some big numbers with a big black sharpie on the work sheet and told you "make it happen" and you made it happen and the vehicle was sold.

The dealership owner or his puppet general manager who are making most of the profit from your work did not even see this customer and did not call to thank them for their business and they did not even send this customer a thank you card with their own signature. You have done it but dealer deduct a few dollars of your commission for their customer relation employee to send a thank you card on the dealership's behalf.

I told you before that manufactures do not give a shit about salesmen and one of the reasons is this:

Manufactures push their dealers to have a business development center (BDC) but never question their dealers who is paying for it?

Why salesmen must pay for the car dealer customer relation employee's wages or salary? Why they have to kiss customers asses for the fucking lazy dealer to get the award?

Anyway, you have done everything from start to finish and what did you get? A mini commission of $50 to $100 or about 20% or 25% commission of the front end gross profit after the pack, and dealer gets to keep over 75% or more of the profit.

The sales manager tells you that you have no right to see the invoice or look at the computer and since you cannot see anything you cannot be sure that what you are getting is really what your pay plan or your verbal agreement says.

You really cannot tell if dealer is paying you 25%, 15%, 10% or even 7%. Nobody is showing you anything, you just have to take their word for it and accept whatever they give you. If you insist on looking at your own deal, they accuse you of not trusting them.

These fucking crooks do not trust you to see anything but they want you to trust and accept their word. What kind of bullshit is that?

What's even funnier is as long as everything is smooth and the customer is happy with you and the deal, that customer is known as dealers customer but if some thing goes wrong and somehow or some- where customer finds out that he/she got screwed in that deal either by the sales manager or finance manager, or if they found a dent or a chip in the paint or if the check engine light keep coming on and the service department keep running them around, suddenly that unhappy customer becomes "your customer" and you have to handle the heat even if you absolutely had nothing to do with it.

Your CSI score goes down and the crooked dealer who is always looking for excuses to steal some more of your money will deduct another fifty or more dollars from your paycheck and then starts fucking with the little bonuses that you may qualify for.

Dealers have a saying of "what you don't know, won't hurt you" and that works for them very well. If a salesperson sees that car dealer is screwing with his commission, he/she will not work for the asshole and since dealers know that they do not let salesmen see anything just in case they may figure it out.

The sales department closes at 7 pm on Sundays and you met the customer about six o'clock and the sold unit was delivered and hit the curb a little after nine o'clock, more than two hours after the closing time. Do you think you did a good job and also do you think it was a good and smart business move from your side? Sales manager said that you did a good job making him and the dealer money and made yourself few dollars commission.

Yes, I agree. You did a good job by convincing the customer that you are the right salesperson to buy this vehicle from but what about your real commission?

We always do a good job as a salesmen when we use our talent and salesmanship to sell a vehicle, but do we get our fair share of the commission?

The car dealer puts his money in as an investment but not his time. You put your time in as an investment and since "time is money" that means you both have equal investment in the deal. Why do you get 20% and that weasel gets 80%? In most cases it is not even the dealers investment, he is flooring it. What is wrong with this picture?

The dealer has invested his own or the banks' money, you have done all of the work by putting in your time and using your sales talent. Aren't you partners? Because of you selling the unit he is making money from the front and the back end of that deal.

You were the salesman and because of you selling the unit, he is making several hundred dollars 'hold back' money that the manufacturer is giving him and again, you do not get any part of that money either.

The customer bought the unit because you convinced them to buy. You were the reason for every kind of profit that the dealer made in front end, back end, hold back and documentation fee on that transaction. Why are you getting so little and he is keeping so much? Why won't he let you see if you are really getting that 20%? Why every deal in the car dealerships is being kept secret from the salesmen?

Any kind of verbal, written or contractual agreement should be for both parties and each party must have the right to make sure that the other is responsible and honors his or her obligation.

These crooks want to see and make sure that salesmen are upholding their end of the deal. They want to see what we are doing and make sure everything is in black and white on our side but they do not want us to know or see anything on their side.

If they pay you salary or hourly wages I don't care, but you are paid commission and you should have the right to know if they are paying you the correct commission.

Every one of these untrustworthy crooks wants us to just take their fucking word for it and we all know that a thief's words do not mean shit.

Why dealers have the right to control everything but salesmen do not have the right to see anything? Again, what kind of bullshit is that?

My fellow salespeople, I showed you already that your bosses are crooks and thieves and they do not trust or respect you, how do you expect the society to trust and respect you when your own arrogant bosses do not?

Please get another job and let these crooked assholes sell their own fucking vehicles and type their own fucking deals unless this crooked and corrupted system take steps in the right direction otherwise they will keep screwing you over and over again.

If you are waiting for a miracle to happen and things to get better like I told you before, miracles do not happen in the car dealerships.

If things get better, they are getting better for these crooked con artists not for you or me. Things are not going to change unless we change them. In fact they are getting worse and you are feeling it everyday that goes by.

You are working in one of the most fucked up and corrupted industries that have been giving their salesmen pay cuts instead of pay raises for several decade and to make the matters worse they have been doing it with a silencer called the "pack" smoothly and quietly.

The only raise for the salespeople in this fucked up business is the raise in the pack not raise in the commission. Any experience salesperson knows that.

These crooked weasels have no dignity, no shame and most of all, they have no fucking balls to be straight and tell their salesmen/women that they are getting "pay cuts" whenever they want to raise the pack.

They play it just like con artists and call for mandatory sales meetings, then they set up the stage and talk about inflation and cost of gas, rent, utilities, blah, blah, blah, and keep schmoozing salespeople. After one hour of bullshit, they finally spit it out and making it sound like they are still doing the salespersons a favor by paying them the same 20% or 25% commission, but due to the inflation and a raised cost of living pack went up only $100.

They don't have the fucking balls to say that they raised the pack and you are getting pay cuts, they 'con' you into it.

If their excuse for raising the pack is inflation they need to understand that their salespeople get hurt more by inflation than the fucking dealer.

If the price of gas went up 30 cents per gallon, salesmen get hurt a lot more than the fucking car dealers. Salesmen only have one source of income and that is 20% or 25% commission of the front end gross profit after the pack, but car dealers make all kinds of profits.

They keep the pack plus over 75% of the front end gross of each deal and that is only if they did not steal anything from the front end of the deals, they keep an average of over 85% of the profit of the back end gross and again, if they are not packing the real cost for their finance managers, they get to keep all of the hold back, incentives and bonuses that manufacturers are giving them.

Their parts and service departments are making them money and there are other kickbacks that salespeople do not know any thing about and they also make profit from the trade ins that they sell at the auctions or to the wholesalers and addition to all of the above, believe it or not, every year they make several thousand dollars (some dealers make several hundred thousand dollars) profit just from the "documentation fees" which they do not pay any commission on.

I am not bullshitting you. I once saw a salesman made $75 mini commission on a deal but the dealer made over $7000 profit from the back end of that deal. The profits that they make from the front and back end of some deals far outweigh what the salesmen make.

Only God knows how many deals like that happen in car dealerships every day. The salesperson keep getting screwed and can not do anything about it.

The ass kissing sales manager runs to his boss or bosses and makes himself a hero. The cocksucker acts like he is the one who created the deal and wants to get credit for his salespeople performance.

These are the things that are pissing me off in the auto sales industry. It is proven fact that if a customer doesn't like the sales person, he/she will make some sort of excuse and leave that car lot.

The salesman has to sell himself to the customer first, then sell the vehicle. Do you think it is fair that the working sales person makes $75 and the lazy fucking asshole who was not even there, makes over $7000.

If the crook were to put his money in the bank instead of opening a car dealership the maximum interest he could have made from the bank was less than 5%.

Give me a fucking break asshole. Gas prices did not just go up for you, it hurt salesmen too, utility costs did not just go up for you, they went up for salesmen also and inflation hurts everyone not just you stupid fucking son of the bitch.

As a salesman you may say that you have no other choice and there isn't a better job out there. That is fine and I do not see anything wrong in selling cars and making an honest living, but remember, a good car salesman is the one who takes control of the customers and does not let customers control him.

A good salesman does not let his time being wasted by jack offs and a good salesman does not put up with lying, double crossing, cheating and two faced dealers.

Nobody likes to sell vehicles and put up with bullshit. We all work hard for our money. We are out there in the heat or cold, rain or shine. We put in lots of time, we put up with a lot of jack offs that waste our time. We listen to lots of bullshit and lies from customers and our own bosses and we get screwed by manufacturers for ride and drive, CSI, certified bullshit and the BDC.

It is time to unite and tell these scumbags to wake up and smell the coffee. Heydays are over and if you want me to sell your products pay the fair share otherwise, "take your fucking job and shove it."

Individually we cannot do anything. If one, two or even five salesmen raise their voices and the dealer feels that his control is in jeopardy, the dealer will fire all of them on the spot to make an example for others.

They all show you the greener grass but as soon as you start working for them the same shit will happen and you will keep getting screwed over and over and there's no end to it.

Comfortable living is good for everybody not just for these lazy fucking assholes who are living in their big fancy homes and are on vacation more than nine months of the year.

A lot of these con artists do not even have a clock or calendar in their houses to see what time or what day of the week it is, every day is a fucking holiday to them.

They wake up when they feel like it and go to sleep when they feel like it. They eat and drink whenever they want to and they screw whenever their greed gets to the boiling point and they don't give a shit about you or customers and sometime they do not even give a shit about the law.

To them you are just a number in the dealership and you are only as good as the number of the vehicles that you are selling.

Their general managers and sales managers have been trained that way too and their whole goal is to keep their bosses happy and keep those big checks coming.

There is no pride or dignity within their circle and there is no manhood left for them.

What kind of a man would sell himself for the money? They are not man. Having a few inches between their legs does not make them a man. Dogs have that too, donkeys have three times more, but dogs or donkeys do not lie, do not cheat and do not steal from others like these fucking crooked dealers, their ass kissing general managers, cock sucking sales managers and compulsive liar closers do.

All victims of crooked dealers should keep in mind the old saying "fool me once, shame on me, fool me twice shame on me fool me three times, fuck you."

You dealers have been forcing your salespeople to consistently lie to customers for over eighty years and they have been getting the blame for it. Car salesmen do not have a good reputation in American society because of you fucking con artists.

You have been collecting the money and they have been collecting the blame for your dirty games and now it is time for the car salespeople to say fuck you!

Car dealers are cash cows for the cities and counties and they create lots of revenue for Department of Motor Vehicles. Do not expect city, county, or the state to go after them if they are cheating you on your fair share of commission. Do not go to the labor board and ask for justice. The law is on their side, they've got the money and we all know that "money talks."

Years ago a very famous attorney said, "the color of justice is not black or white, It is green."

We all have seen how famous people with money who've committed crimes have gotten away with it. In some famous cases they have gotten away with actual murder.

We all have had more than enough of the car dealer's bullshit over the last several decades and it is time to do something about it and please, please, please, lets do it now and do it together otherwise, these crooked con artists will keep screwing us over and over and over and over and over and over…

Chapter four

GENERAL MANAGERS

"Over 99 percent of car dealers give the rest a bad name."

A TYPICAL GENERAL MANAGER OF A FRANCHISE car dealership goes to work whenever he feels like it and parks his demo in the shadiest spot closest to the building.

Before closing the door he pulls out his briefcase giving the impression that he's so busy that he has to take his work home every night. No one knows what's in that briefcase, probably nothing, as no one's allowed to ask him.

If yesterday was a good day and a few vehicles were sold, the sales manager will be looking forward to see the general manager in order to tell him the good news.

The morning shift sales manager will drop whatever he was doing and runs outside to the parking lot to meet the boss at his car door. He keeps his brown nosing and tries to get credit for the hard work that the poor salespeople have done.

Salesmen sold the vehicles, finance managers sold the garbage in the back end but the stupid ass kisser monkey who only punched some numbers in the computer is trying to make a hero out of himself.

He even takes the print out report of yesterdays sales with him outside to show his boss that what he has done.

He is acting just like a dog seeing his owner, cannot hide his excitement and keeps trying to get credit for the hard work of the salespeople to himself.

On the other hand, if it has been slow over the course of the last few days and If the dealership went blank yesterday and did not sell anything, the sales manager does not even want to see the bosses face.

He keeps praying that the GM is at the golf course again, calls in sick or his wife forced him to go shopping with her. He just does not want to witness the GM's bad mood.

If the general manager starts walking toward the sales office, the sales manager makes sure that the lot is covered and the rest of the salesmen are on the phone doing their follow ups and making appointments.

The ass kisser keeps rehearsing to himself of what excuses can he use this time? He needs good reasons for not having any sales and why the sales department went blank on his shift. He knows that car dealers and their general managers do not want to hear any excuses.

They pay their dumb asses sales managers several thousand dollars from the hard work of the salespeople every month and they do not want to hear any excuses.

The general manager goes to his big fancy office which has the best heating and air conditioning in the house, takes his coat off and sits behind his fancy desk. He turns on the computer and looks at the numbers.

He wants to know profits from sales, finance, part and service departments just in case if the owner calls and questions him.

This would take about ten minutes and then he looks at the heat sheet. It is not that he is too lazy to walk a few feet to the finance department or business office to see what deals have not been funded from the banks. He calls the finance director or the business manager to his office just to show that he is in charge, he has control and wants to know what is going on with those deals.

He may bark at any department manager that did not sell enough of parts, services or vehicles yesterday over the phone a few minutes or may even call the head of those departments to his office and shake them up a little bit. He listens to his answering machine and may return a few phone calls, and it is time for lunch.

He usually goes to lunch with some banks' rep and buys their lunch in a fancy restaurant on the company's credit card and gets them to buy the C or D papers deeper. Or he may take a manufacturers rep to lunch to help him out with his inventory and some hard to get units or he may do it just to make friend with the factory rep for the future.

After his two hours lunch break is over, he goes back to his office where a pretty girl from a bank, insurance company, news paper or some stupid internet site is waiting to sell him something. Since she is pretty and money is not coming out of the general managers own pocket, he may lay down and buys whatever she is selling in hopes of getting into this pretty girls' pants one day.

It is so obvious that lots of companies are using sexy females to sell their products to car dealers. They know how un-ethical car dealers or their general managers are.

These girls are trained so well that when they drive into a car lot you can smell their perfume before they even open their car doors. They have half of their breast out of their bra and that will catch the attention of every salesperson. As soon as she gets out of her car, male employees start drooling like pit bull dogs.

No soliciting signs do not mean shit anymore. These girls have done their homework so well that within twenty five minutes they have sold their products and have the horny general manager thinking that he is going to get into their pants very soon.

The monkey face general manager doesn't know that after signing the contract with this pretty lady the next rep will be another face and another tactic and he will never get a chance to get to that saleslady's pants. He can only stick his dick in his own imagination.

Whenever a pretty female is selling something, car dealers or their managements are lay downs and that is the reason that most of the banks, insurance companies, news papers, warranty companies, alarm companies, advertising, internet companies or any after market company try to use attractive female salespersons to sell their products to the car dealers.

Anyway, the general manager buys whatever she is selling and after she is gone, there's really nothing else to do. He calls his wife and acts like he has been very busy all day but he managed to find a few seconds to tell her I love you, blah, blah, blah.

He gets bored playing monopoly or watching porn on the computer and decides to go outside to get some fresh air.

The evening shift sales manager sees him outside and he does not want to stay behind of the morning shift sales manager so he runs outside and starts kissing the bosses ass too.

The general manager really has nothing new to say but comes in to show that he is watching everything he talks to the evening shift sales manager, expresses some stupid repeated opinion to him and as usual, he gets bored of the ass kisser brown nosing and goes back to his office and plays a little more games on his computer.

Finally he turns the computer off, picks up the same briefcase acting like he has not finished the days business yet, gets in to his demo that has been filled up with the company's credit card by the lot porter already and leaves.

If his wife is not going to chew his ass out he may stop at a bar for a drink or two and goes home to tell his wife "what a rough day he had."

He puts on the busy man act again but this time the act is on his own family.

He takes the briefcase to his home office and sits behind the computer again and gets on line to chat with only God knows who and he may even play some more games.

The poor wife is busting her butt trying to make a nice dinner for her money making husband. She keeps trying to quiet the kids, telling them that their father is still occupied with his work and he is busy in the home office.

Finally the actor comes out and ready to eat, but as a habit of bullshitting he wants to tell his teen age kids about the reality of life and how hard they have to work to make as much money as he is making, blah, blah, blah.

There is an old saying "If you do not have anything nice to say, just don't say any thing and shut the fuck up," but that rule does not work for some car dealers or their general managers. They are so used to non stop bullshitting that it does not matter who they are bullshitting anymore.

They just love to hear themselves talk, no matter what kind of bullshit they are talking about and it never crossed their stupid fucked up minds that they are talking garbage and boring the hell out of others.

95% of what is being said in the car dealers repetitive sales meetings is bullshit and the other 5% is more bullshit. They are all repeated reminders about how to screw customers to make more front or back end gross.

Car dealers have been bullshitting customers and employees for so long that it becomes a habit to them and when they go home they want to start doing the same shit with their own family members too.

I worked in an RV dealership once to see if they were different from car dealers, they were not and in fact they were worse. I wondered if they treat their customers or employees any better than car dealers, it was a lot worse or at least the one that I worked for was.

Every Monday through Friday the sales meeting and BDC was like a bible class to that RV dealer. We did not have a female salesperson but one of his asshole sales managers was calling the salesmen "ladies." He would put them down just like they were nobody, threat them like animals and kept farting in the sales meeting every time. To that stupid, arrogant asshole it was funny but no one was laughing.

The owner of that RV dealership liked to train his salesmen to become some kind of mind reader. Salesmen were told to turn their customer over to another salesman who has the same attitude and personality as that customer. That was why every salesman had to take a personality test before their employment with that RV dealership.

Every salesperson must turn his customer over to another salesperson as soon as the customer gives him a negative sign. He must report that customers personality to the floor manager and floor manager would decide which salesman he needs to turn that customer to?

Sometimes one customer would end up talking to three different salesmen, floor manager, sales manager and even the general manager before they left the lot.

That RV dealer was putting so much pressure on customers to make them "buy now" than any fucking desperate Joe Blow used car lot.

I worked in the trailer side and never saw any invoice, reconditioning cost or anything that would show that I was getting the correct commission, Just like crooked car dealers I had to take their words for it.

All I know is that I sold a used 5th wheel to a customer and the same asshole farting sales manager told me "good job" and my commission voucher was $1840 but when I got my paycheck the commission on that deal was reduced to just a little over $1400. I got screwed over $400 on that deal.

I quit right away without telling any one in that RV dealership. They called me a few times and finally they got the message that I was done with that fucked up toilet.

They owed me one more check for another deal and after calling them four times and getting jerked around, I finally called the owner and his secretary mailed it to me. That check was over $120 short too.

I worked for that RV dealership over three months. In that time I saw few things that could made car dealers to look like "Mother Teresa" compare to them. One was, cornering customers real hard to "buy now." Others were discrimination from the sales manager toward the salesmen and customers and another one was controlling. I realized that the management in that RV dealership were controlling every move that their salesmen were making.

Turning customers to other salesmen or the floor manager was a must. Putting the customers information in the computer was another must. Follow up on customers until they "buy or die" was something else, and finally going to the fucking BDC room every day and listen to the same bullshit from that farting asshole really bored the hell out of every salesman.

The owner of the dealership loved to talk. Talking was one thing and getting him to shut the fuck up was another thing.

I was in two of his once a month sales meetings and after the dinner he just went on and on and on for over an hour and half. Bullshit after bullshit after bullshit. Almost half of the people in the room were asleep but he would not stop. In fact, he admitted that he is boring the hell out of everyone but he would still not stop.

I quit there and started at another RV and boat dealership with the base salary plus the bonus.

I would never forget the abnormal and bizarre way that the owner was treating his employees including his own sons that were working for him.

He was the most peculiar person that I have ever seen or met in my life. Very smart businessman but extremely controlling, hard headed and selfish. Even his own sons were saying that their father is fucking asshole. To make the story short he had more respect for his dog than anybody including his own sons that were working for him. I worked there about two and half years, and still today, I keep asking myself, why did I put up with that much bullshit that long?

Chapter five

Sales managers

"Over 99 percent of car dealers give the rest a bad name."

As I said at the beginning, it is harder to stay being sales manager than to become a sales manager. Why is that?

To become a sales manager all you have to do is keep making friends with the bosses and keep buying them breakfast and lunches. Take them out for drinks and start planting the seeds. Keep promising that you will do exactly what they want you to do.

Tell them, I'm the best man for the job. I know how to motivate the salespeople and making all kinds of promises. Anything to convince them that you can make a good sales manager.

From the little that I know this kind of act is called "ass kissing."

It is very true in the car business that "If you don't ask, you don't get" but asking and ass kissing are two different things. Ass kissers get to their positions by whoring themselves and sleeping their way up.

Ass kisser managers have no dignity and no pride. Since they have given false promises to their bosses to get the job, they will do anything to keep it.

If the boss wants them to do illegal things they will do it and if the boss asks them to lie and cheat and steal for him they will do it. They completely become puppets and dance to any music that their bosses play. They will have no balls to stand up for their own rights or anyone else' right.

One of the sales managers jobs is to desk the deals and they do not have to be a rocket scientist to do that. You can teach a monkey to desk deals and he can do it, but managing the salespeople in fair and correct way without cheating and showing them how to sell cars and be successful without putting them down and bullshitting them is not a job that everybody can do.

No matter how big the paychecks are, a managers dignity should be bigger because those big paychecks are from the hard work of the salespeople.

A sales manager who has confidence in his managing ability will stand up to his bosses and let them know right from wrong even if it may cost him his job in that store. He knows that he is better off not to work for thieves and crooks.

There is no job security working for thieves anyway. First, they make you steal from others and put it in their pockets and then they start stealing from you and by then you are a party in their crime and that is when karma comes into play for, if it is ok for you to steal from others, it should be ok for the boss to steal from you as well.

Greed has no limit and nothing stops greedy car dealers from screwing others including their employees, sales managers are not excluded either.

In fact car dealers have already been stealing from their sales managers for many years on the reconditioning costs of the used vehicles and hidden packs on accessories but as far as I know, no sales managers had the balls to say or do anything about it.

To the car dealers greedy eyes, a good sales manager is the one who has more gross profit per deal. To them "he is strong."

There are reasons why most of the management jobs in different companies require management trainee, university or a college degree. Being a manager is not just to order others to do this or that. It takes a lot of talent, creativity and in the mean time a manager should know how to talk to the employees, bosses and customers. Over all a manager should know what is right, fair and correct for every body.

In car dealerships, sales managers do what their kinky car dealer or his/her puppet general manager wants them to do but again, most car dealers do not have any education themselves and some of them can not even talk if you take the "F" word out of their mouth.

Car dealers do not want their sales managers to know too much anyway, and they do not want salesmen to know nothing at all because, turnover for sales managers, closers and salespeople is huge and there is a good chance that someone might blow the whistle on them. The less everyone knows the better it is for the dealer.

What amazes me is that every sales manager knows all of this, but they have no balls to tell their bosses, let the salespeople make their correct commission and do not make us steal from them.

Years ago, I was working with a salesman who hated the general manager and the owner of the dealership that we were both selling vehicles at. He knew that they were screwing us bad and every time he passed by the general managers' office door, he spit on the doorknob and said "fucking thief."

Few years later he got promoted to be finance manager, he was one of the kinkiest finance managers that I have ever seen in my life but still had the same attitude toward the owner, general manager and sales managers, but he just turned 180 degrees when they promoted him to the sales manager position.

He became the best ass kisser and snitch for the same general manager and the owner that he was calling all kinds of names before. To this day, I can guarantee that if they take a lab test from that doorknob or the door, they can find his saliva there.

Just until a few days before he became sales manager, he was bitching, complaining and m effing every sales manager, general sales manager, general manager and the owner of that dealership.

He was saying that they are screwing us. Sales managers are all cock suckers and the general manager and the owner are both thieves. Everything is packed and we all are getting fucked, but when he became sales manager, this two faced con artist became a puppet for the same general manager and the owner of the same dealership that he was m effing. If he was told to jump, he would say how high?

This ass kisser showed himself to be as phony as a "three dollar bill."

He completely forgot who he was and how they were treating him before. Right from the get go he started stealing from the salesmen's front end gross per his bosses orders and puts it in the back end.

They bought him out just like millions of other car sales managers in the auto sales industry. He sold himself and changed color like a fucking "chameleons." No one in that dealership could believe that this is the same guy.

We all know that "money talks" but in his case it was like on his first day being sales manager they dropped him in a septic tank and brought him back out because after that day every sales person knew that this asshole is full of shit now.

The same old general manager and the owner became his bible. What is funny is that he used to call other sales managers "cock suckers" but he became one of the best snitch and cock sucker himself.

Sales managers like that two faced asshole are reasons that dishonest dealers and their crooked general managers can do whatever they want and get away with it. They know that they can buy dignity with money, they can buy pride with money and they can keep their sales managers mouths shut with money.

Fair is fair and let it be that way. If you see an employee steals from the dealer, you let the dealer know and if you find out that dealer is stealing from employees, make it clear to him/her that you will let the employees know.

You are sales manager not the general manager or the owner's puppet and you are not their bitch. They do not own you and you should not allow them to buy your dignity.

If a few sales managers had the balls to stand up to their dishonest car dealers or their puppet general managers and let them know that they will not cheat, steal, or lie for them all of this bullshit would stop.

Everybody would be making their fair share of commission and I did not have to write this book. But there are a lot of selfish, arrogant, ignorant, dishonest, and asshole sales managers out there that don't give a shit about anyone but themselves. As long as they are making those big paychecks, they do not give a shit about the others.

My fellow salespeople, don't let these crooked dealers force you to stand up out side of their buildings in a one 100-degree temperature to sell their fucking vehicles while they are having fun being with their families and friends.

Don't let these lazy jackasses make you unlock their car doors every morning and lock them at night. Don't let them make you blow up balloons. You are not their lot porters. Tell the owner and his ass kissing general manager, sales managers and closers to open and lock the vehicles and blow up their fucking balloons.

When you applied for a salesman job at their dealership, no one said anything about opening or locking up their cars, no one told you about their fucking mandatory sales meetings and no one told you that they will take away some part of your front end gross, inflate the reconditioning cost of used vehicles and keep raising the pack.

Every one of these cock sucking sales managers or closers will make you believe that the grass is greener on their side but when you step your foot in to their fucking doors you will see that these ass kissers are all full of shit.

They have been lying, cheating and misleading their salespeople and customers for years and no one has been able to stop them yet.

Dealers have been buying their way through the system for so many years and because their revenue creates a lot of tax money for cities, counties and the state, they get a lot of special and unfair treatment for their fraudulent acts.

We are just like prostitutes for these fucking pimps. We are getting fucked and they are collecting the money and acting like they are not happy and keep pushing their sales managers to screw us more and more.

We should not be the bitches for these fucking assholes, their general managers and sales managers or closers.

If you are waiting for the government to help us, keep waiting. If you are waiting for the Department of Motor Vehicles to help us, keep waiting and if you are waiting for the labor department to help us, keep waiting.

Chapter six

FAIR COMMISSION

"Over 99 percent of car dealers
give the rest a bad name."

I HAVE BEEN TELLING YOU A LOT about getting our fair share of
commission but I haven't told you exactly what I mean by that
yet.

The fair share of commission between salespeople and car dealers
should be 50% of the whole profit including, holdbacks, incentive
and any kind of bonuses that car manufacturers are giving to their
franchise dealers with no pack, plus the minimum wage.

Salesmen deserve 50% of the whole profit of the front end gross
plus 50% of holdbacks, incentives and bonuses on every new vehicle.
They also deserve 50% of the front end gross profit on every used
vehicle including the trade ins that they sell to the wholesalers or at
the auctions.

Things like "pack, inventory charge, inflation adjustment or other bullshit" that these fucking con artist are imposing on the salespeople should have never been there to begin with.

I know car dealers very well and if we do not get 50% of the hold backs or cash incentives and bonuses they can make their franchise head quarters to shrink the profit margin from the MSRP to invoice and put it in the hold backs, incentives or bonuses for them and again, salespeople get screwed.

We all know that car manufacturers or their headquarters do not give a shit about the salespeople. They only care about their customers which are their franchise dealers. They only want the salesmen to sell their vehicles and finance managers to sell their warranty, gap, auto care and other bullshit. Then they push their franchise dealers to punish us for having the low CSI.

Do not feel like 50% commission plus the minimum wage is too much. Remember that we are doing the work and these jack asses are on non stop vacation and again, if these crooks put their money in the bank, the return for their investment is less than 5%.

With 50% no pack pay plan plus the minimum wage, dealers are still making 50% of the front end gross of each deal and they still get to keep 50% of the money from the back end and also do not forget that they are making several thousand dollars in their part and service departments every month. (several hundred thousand dollars in some stores) and they make thousands of dollars from the "documentation" fees.

Documentation fees are another tricky way that these con artists came up with to make more "non-commissionable" profit from their customers. These con artists do really know how to make profit without any labor cost and have it down to an art.

They charge every customer a "doc fee" by making them believe that this is an official fee and at the same time they use the "pack" for their salesmen and make them believe that is the cost of doing business.

These con artists really know how to move up the ladders without even buying a ladder. I have to give it to them. They have found so many ways to get customers and salesmen to pay their fucking bills. What a smart and genius way to do business. They just have it designed so prefect by fooling customers, employees, government, banks and everyone else.

Finance managers also deserve 50% of everything that they sell in back end of the deals because, they put in a lot of time and overtime, and they do all of the pitch to sell the crap to the customers.

Why do they do all the work and give over 85% of their hard work to the fucking dealers? After all, car dealers do not have any investment what so ever in a lot of the garbage that their finance managers are selling any way.

My fellow salespeople, we all deserve a lot more pay for the jobs that we do and the hours that we put in at these corrupted dealerships. If your bosses read this book they will try to make jokes about me. They will say that I am a dreamer and they will keep making jokes about 50% no pack plus the minimum wage, but the day will come and then the jokes will be on them.

Do not let your sales managers or closers fool you. Do not let your general manager threaten you with your job. You do not have a job, it is only an opportunity to sell their fucking vehicles.

Read your pay plans again. You will see that 99% is to their advantage and the other 1% is leaning toward their sides too.

Deep in their hearts, closers, sales managers and even general managers know that I am right, but they cannot open their mouths and relay that to their bosses.

Again, I am not bullshitting you, they put in their money and we are putting in our time and sales talents. It must be 50/50.

With this pay plan car dealers would not have to grease their sales managers or general managers anymore because there would be no more covering up.

They do not have to pay their master thieves general managers $40,000 a month for being twenty hours at the dealership and thirty hours at the golf courses every week.

Selling car is not as easy as it sounds. It takes a lot of patience, skills, talent, and most of all discipline.

It is not easy to change a shopper to a buyer and convince them to cough up10, 20, 30, 50 or more thousand dollars without letting them go home and think about it or sleep it over.

Selling cars is not like the counter selling that you see in car rentals, hotels, drug stores, gas stations, auto parts or fast food places. There are lots of negotiation and salesmanship involved and salespeople must be prepared for the customers lies and other bullshit excuses. Challenge and over come them.

When you get a prospect you are the one who starts running from one side of the lot to the other side to land them on the right vehicle. You are the one who do the walk around. You are the one who takes them on demo ride and put your own life at the risk without knowing who is in the driver seat? What kind of back ground or driving records do they have?

You are the one who is selling yourself and convincing that customer to come inside and you are the one who is doing the negotiations and overcoming their excuses to sell them the vehicle.

You are the one who fills up the credit application, copy their insurance card and driver license, takes the customer to finance, fills up the gas tank, put the vehicle in the wash rack, put RS on the windshield and explain the fixtures and futures and deliver the vehicle and finally you are the one who the CSI is pointing at.

You have done all of that while the car dealer is asleep or is having good time with his family and friends.

Please don't tell me that you do not deserve 50% of that deal.

The lazy dealer and his ass kissing general manager were not even there while you were doing all of the work but later on they will complain that you are not selling enough units or sold that vehicle too cheap and left some money on the table. Just to say something and show you that they are in control.

You want to tell the son of a bitch "If you don't have anything nice to say, shut the fuck up and don't say anything," but you just have to keep biting your tongue and say nothing.

I am sure that there have been lots of complains about car

dealers fraudulent acts, discrimination, sexual harassment, unfair labor practices, dishonesty and other DMV violations in different courthouses around the country already. I have seen it on the TV read about it in the newspapers and heard it on the radio.

Joe Blow dealership was shut down because he was inflating customers incomes on the credit applications, but soon the jack ass is back in business as if nothing has ever happened.

The crooked dealer and his ass kisser general manager are the main reasons behind of all of the fraud but they fire a few members of the sales team and play a little house ninety with the city, county and the state officials, pay few dollars fine and reopen again.

After a few weeks people forget and everything is back to normal and the con artist resume his fraudulent bullshit.

Car dealers and their manufactures advertise a lot on the TV and radio stations. They put lots of ad in the local newspapers and most of these media points are afraid to lose the dealer or the car makers business if they report them or say or write something negative about their fraudulent acts.

To give you an example, In August 2009 an off duty California highway patrol officer and his three family members were killed in a car accident. His 911 call saying his vehicle is out of control and he can not stop it was heard by millions of people later on from different radio and TV stations saying "It has reached speeds of up to 120 mph" before hitting another vehicle and went through a fence off the freeway, rolled several times and then caught fire. He, his wife, their 13 year old daughter and his brother-in-law all died in that crash.

The car maker blamed the faulty floor mat but if you look at the year and model of that vehicle you will notice that driver side floor mat is supported by a hook on the floor and can not move unless you unhook it, even then, floor mats do not climb up the gas pedals. There were recall after recall for a short while and then no news about it at all.

After a few days, that car manufacture started advertising in the news papers and on the radio and TV stations again.

The point is, whether it was the floor mat or electronic throttle control system we are not hearing it on the radio any more, we are not seeing it on the TV any more and we are not reading about it in the news papers any more.

Money talks, bullshit walks, but this was not bullshit. Four people lost their lives because of a car manufactures fuck up. Similar accidents had happened before this one from the same car manufacture but they were brushed under the rug. The media did not want to lose the advertise money that they were making from this car maker.

In the future you may hear or see a few seconds news about this car maker settling with the family of the victims but what about the people who lost their lives? What did they get? Each one got a grave six feet under the ground.

If the media had reported the truth to begin with and did not let go until this car manufacture get their shit together and fix the problem with their fucking floor mats or electronic throttles, these four people would have not lost their lives.

To the medias' bosses, news will stay on peoples mind for a short time then starts fading away and people forget, but this car maker will cut us off out of millions of dollars of advertisement if we keep talking or writing about it. Do you honestly think that is fair?

I have seen things in the sales and finance departments of car dealerships that will blow your minds away;

Years ago, I started working at one car dealer in Southern California but I was not told that they have forty nine retail salesmen and five fleet and internet managers. They were selling an average of 350 vehicles a month with that many salespeople. I quit that toilet just a few hours after I started.

I have worked at car dealership that had a hawk man spying on the salesmen on the lot with a binocular and I worked at one car dealership that was forcing their salesmen and women to hold hands and pray for the owner of the dealership and his business every day before their shift started. I was told that general sales manager was pastor in some church also.

Believe it or not, that general sales manager had the highest gross average than any deskman that I know of. His philosophy was "always go for the jugular."

I have seen dealers eavesdropping on their salesmen or even tape their telephone conversations. Once a while they would bring the tape to the sales meetings and let other sales people listen to it and make fun of the poor spying target. There really is no privacy or respect for the sales people from the management, It's all about control.

Chapter seven

PACK

"Over 99 percent of car dealers
give the rest a bad name."

THERE ARE TWO TYPES OF PACK in the car and RV dealerships, regular pack and hidden Pack.

The first few hundreds of dollars of the front end gross profit that dealers make and do not pay any commission on to their salespeople is called "regular pack."

The dealers excuse for the regular pack is, salesmen must pay a part of our advertisement, flooring, rent, utilities, office employees and porters wages too.

Inflating the cost of repairing used vehicles or RVs and jacking up the cost for accessories and invoices are known as the "hidden Pack."

The amount of regular pack varies from dealer to dealer and is based on their greed, pay plans and model of vehicles or RVs. It may be from $100 to $5000 or even more per unit.

Some dealers call it pack, some call it inflation adjustment and some even call it inventory charge. I call it "control"

Usually dealers have pack for their retail salespersons but some have pack for their fleet and internet managers and some of them even have packs on some of the items that their finance managers sell in the back end of the deals.

I have never seen a dealer having pack for their sales managers although indirectly they pack the shit out of reconditioning cost of their used vehicles and accessories which will affect the sales and finance managers earnings a lot.

Why do car dealers have pack for the commissioned salespeople? The answer is, "control."

We all know that every employee expect to get raise after being with the same company for a while.

Car dealers can simply have no pack and hire a salesman at 20% commission and a year later raise the commission to 21% and two years later to 22%, and on and on. After fifteen years of being with the same dealership that salespersons' commission is 35% and after twenty years he/she is getting 40% of the front end gross, but car dealers don't like that.

As greedy, kinky, crooked and full of shit as these scumbags are, that is a big no- no to them because they don't have the balls to tell their commissioned salespeople, we are not giving you any pay raise. You only get pay cut, so they came up with a tricky way of screwing their commissioned salesmen's earnings and called it the "pack."

I will show you how the pack benefit the dealers:

Just suppose Jim started working at Joe Blow car lot as a car salesman in 1985 with 20% commission after the $50 pack. Twenty years later in 2005 his commission has not gone up but the pack has. His 20% commission stayed the same but the pack kept going up during the years and is $700 now.

What this means is, if Jim sold a car back in 1985 and his front end gross profit was $2,000 after the $50 pack, he made 20% commission on $1950 which was $390.

The same front end gross happens twenty years later but the pack has gone up to $700 now which leaves $1,300 payable to Jim and 20% commission of that is $260.

This is a loss of $130 commission on the same front end gross deal to Jim after 20 years of employment with the same crooked asshole who had no fucking balls to tell him "the more you work for me, the more I screw you."

Experienced salespeople know how the pack can affect their commissions and know whenever the dealer raises the pack, they are getting pay cut again.

Pack is a silencer that car dealers are using to have the total control to fuck with their salespeople's commissions and reduce it without creating heat.

Let me show you another example, Just suppose you get 25% commission of the front end gross after the pack and six months later your dealer raises the pack by $100 per unit. That means $25 more is deducted from your paycheck on every vehicle that you sell. If you are selling an average of 12 vehicles a month, you just lost 12 X $25 = $300 in one month or $3600 a year.

Like I said before car dealers do not have the fucking balls to be honest with their salespeople and tell them your 25% commission just dropped down. They know that is too obvious and their salesmen will quit on them so, they raise the pack instead.

Usually when car dealers want to raise the pack they buy breakfast for all of the salesmen at that sales meeting and after the breakfast, general manager starts talking about different things and tries to be nice and funny to the salesmen and sets up the stage by telling them that the cost of living has gone up and the company has to adjust for the inflation and blah, blah, blah.

Finally, the master thief spits it out by saying the company was asking for $300 raise in the pack but I kept fighting for you until they dropped it down to only $100.

He makes it looks like only $100 raise in the pack is nothing compared to the on going inflation rate.

The crooked puppet acts like he is on the salesmen side trying to close them on the raising of the pack smoothly, and passes out the new pay plan papers for their signatures knowing that there is no copy machine in the meeting room.

Salesmen have no choice but to sign the new pay plan without really having time to read or even make a copy of it.

If later on you ask for a copy of the new pay plan that you were forced to sign, they will give you a dirty look and tell you, what's the matter? Don't you trust us? If you don't trust us you better start looking for another place to work.

They always turn the stage around and put themselves on the offensive side and put you on the defense side and make you the guilty party. They make you feel bad to even see a copy of your new pay plan.

You may think $100 increase in the pack is not such a big deal but it is very big deal to these greedy crooked con artists and it is all about the "numbers game."

If a car dealer sells an average of 500 vehicles a month in all of his dealerships, raising the pack by only $100 means that he is saving commission on $50,000 a month, and that translates to $600,000 a year. 25% commission of that money is $150,000 that he just screwed his salespeople again.

If that car dealer has a total of 30 sales men, the average salesperson just lost $5000 income in one year.

Pack is the best lubricant that car dealers are using to fuck their commissioned employees.

Crooked dealers have packs all over their dealerships. They have regular pack on new or used vehicles and hidden packs on invoices and other accessories, but the most profitable hidden pack is inflating the costs of repairs on their used vehicles and that is where salesmen, closers, sales managers and general sales managers all get fucked.

Just suppose that a car dealer sells an average of 130 used vehicles a month and the dealer inflates the recondition costs only $1000 average per vehicle. That is an extra income of $130,000 a month which makes $1,560,000 dollars a year.

25% commission on this money is $390,000 that this kinky asshole is screwing his salesmen out of. Sales managers, general sales manager and closers do not make any commissions on that $1,560,000 either.

Every closer, sales manager and general sales manager know that car dealer is screwing them on the commission of that money but they have no balls to say any thing. Their balls have been cut off by the owner or his general manager before they get their titles.

Chapter eight

PREPAID VEHICLE REGISTRATION FEES

MY FINANCIAL BACKGROUND IN THE AUTO sales industry gave me the knowledge to come up with a concept that not only creates millions of dollars for most of the states in the country, it saves them millions of dollars of expenses at the same time too.

The revenue from my concept in each state has to do with two facts:

1 - Number of new vehicles that are financed or leased every year in that state.

2 - The cost of the first year registration and renewal fees that state is charging every year after that.

To understand this concept a little better I will use the State of California as an example.

Since consumers who finance their new vehicles in California can finance the FIRST YEAR of their vehicle registration fees and rolled them into their monthly payments for the total term of their loan, it would benefit everyone if California passed a law that allows consumers to finance the total amount of their vehicle registration fees for the TOTAL TERM of their finance contract and roll them into their monthly payments as well.

In other words, their registration fees has been prepaid until the end of the last year of their finance contract.

According to few sources, California franchise car dealers have sold or leased over 1,290,000 NEW vehicles in 2011 and it was forecasted that the sales will increase in the year 2012.

From these 1,290,000 new vehicles, approximately 10% or 130,000 were sold on the cash basis, about 20% or 260,000 were leased and the other 900,000 were financed.

The average registration fee for new vehicles (cars and pick ups) in the state of California is approximately $400 per unit.

The states' earning from the 900,000 consumers who financed their new vehicle in 2011 was about;

900.000 X $400 = $360,000,000

If California had started my concept from January 2011, by the end of that year the state could have been ahead over 850 million dollars and this is how.

For the year 2011
900,000 x $400 = $360,000,000
Plus the year 2012
900,000 X $320 = $288,000,000
And the year 2013
900,000 X $256 = $230,400,000
And the year 2014
900,000 X $205 = $184,500,000
And the year 2015
900,000 X $164 = $147,600,000
Total of $1,210,500,000

Above numbers which were based on the typical five year vehicle finance contract and the reduction of 20% renewal fee after the year 2011 show that the state could have been ahead over 850 million dollars by the end of that year.

The state could have used the same concept for the normal three year leases and got ahead another 250 million dollars which could jump this over 1.1 billion dollars and if the state had done the same with the used vehicles, RVs, motorcycles, etc, etc, etc, the revenue would easily had grown up close to 1.5 billion dollars in 2011.

These earnings could be realized every year thus continuously helping reduce the State budget deficit. Benefits of this concept are:

1 - This revenue created without any lay offs, raising taxes or putting pressure on the consumers because they must pay this fee every year anyway.

2 - A lot of people are living from paycheck to paycheck and are having a hard time to make their monthly payments and the one time renewal registration fee at the same month, but with my concept they only have one payment a month and do not have to worry about renewing their registrations until their vehicle is paid off or their lease is up.

3 - Consumers know that their vehicle registration fees have been prepaid and will not go up for the next few years.

4 - Very often car manufactures offer zero or very low finance rates which help a lot of consumers to pay none or very little interest for financing the total term of their vehicle registration fees.

5 - The convenience of not dealing with the DMV for few years is a big plus for everyone and may even invite some cash buyers to prepay their registration fees too.

6 - With shorter lines, other clients can do their businesses with the DMV faster.

7 - The state of California can save millions of dollars on the administrative supplies such as, printers, ink, envelopes, papers, stamps and license plate tags.

8 - If the DMV refunds a portion of the balance that is left on the registration back to those who sell or trade in their vehicles before the expiration date of their contract, there would be no excuses for consumers not to sell or trade their vehicles and buy or lease another one to keep the economy moving forward.

Consumers payments increases a few dollars more a month pending on the type of vehicle that they finance or lease but we all know that renewing vehicles' registration is a must and it has to be done every year. It can be prepaid by rolling it into the monthly payments and make the life a lot easier for everyone or be paid by one lump sum once a year just like it is now.

California is only one example here. Other states can use their own calculation to see how much this concept can help them.

This concept will put America ahead by billions of dollars without raising taxes or taking jobs away from anyone.

Car dealers do not like this concept because they want to bump their customers payments by selling them gap, warranty, lo jack, alarm, paint protection, etc, etc. They do not need to be worry, my idea would not slow them down from selling their back end crap in their finance departments.

Vehicle registration fees are already included in the customers payments just like it is now before their customer walk in to the finance office and in fact it would make it easier for their finance managers to sell their back end garbage.

Chapter nine

SOLUTION

'Over 99 percent of car dealers
give the rest a bad name."

AFTER TALKING TO A LOT OF salespeople at different car lots about the pressures that car dealers are putting on them and also the tricks and other kinky shit that dealers are using to screw their sales people out of their fair share of commissions, everyone agreed that individually we can not do anything.

The only solution that we came up with was having the "union."

There are reasons why carpenters, electricians, police officers, fire fighters, sheriff deputies, nurses, janitors, iron workers, city, county and state employees, teachers, most of the grocery stores and even some American car manufacture employees have unions.

Whether you agree or not, union is our only solution but the problem is, dealers do not want their employees to have union. They know the union will set a "fair for everybody" guide line and that will take most of the controls away from them and like I have told you before, dealers are the most controlling employers out there and they do not want to give up any part of that control.

Car dealers blame the unions for car manufactures failures. They are blaming the unions that have the duty to protect their members making few dollars and have some benefits while the CEO's and presidents of these manufactures are making several millions of dollars a year.

Have in mind that some of these hard working employees have been with the same car manufactures about thirty or more years. Bosses want them to take pay cuts but they do not want to have any changes to their own fucking salaries, bonuses, benefits and lifestyles.

Addition to the millions of dollars salary, they want to pay themselves millions of dollars in bonuses for the bad and fucked up management that they have done. They want to keep the time share, yacht, private jet and other benefits to themselves but they want the hard working labors to just drop dead.

That being said, it is too obvious that car dealers who are the puppets for their own franchise automobile manufactures do not want their employees having any kind of protection from the unions.

Car dealers want to keep their 100% control and continue their unfair free labor practices that they have been doing for last several decades in their dealerships in the name of commission and as kinky as they are, they know that union will not allow them to do so anymore.

If a dealer try to pull kinky bullshit tricks like the regular pack or hidden packs, slave driving and using the commissioned salesmen time for nothing, the union will step in and make every sales person in that dealership to go on strike until the problem is solved.

A few days of strike does not hurt a salesperson that much, we all have gone blank for few days but it does have a big impact on the crooked dealers' income.

I am going to show you how much money you are loosing on your paychecks every month on just the regular pack.

If your dealers' regular pack is $500 per vehicle and your commission is 25% of the front end gross after the pack, your dealer is screwing you $125 on every unit that you are selling. If your average sell is 12 vehicles per month that means that the crooked con artist is screwing you out of $1500 a month or $18,000 a year.

This is real money that your crooked dealer is stealing from you in the name of "pack" every year.

if you add the hidden packs on the accessories and specially the reconditioning cost on their used vehicles, you are getting screwed by another $10.000 or more a year.

If you sell an average of 12 new and used vehicles a month, between the regular pack and all of their hidden packs, you are getting screwed about $2500 a month.

Dealers know that the union would put a stop on the regular pack, hidden pack and other kinky shit that they do. Dealers also know that union will force them to pay you according to your pay plan. It may cost about $100 a month to be a union member but you easily gain over $2300 every month.

The choice is yours. If you think I am bullshitting you, stop reading this book and just be the same slave that you have been so far for these fucking slave drivers.

If you believe that what I said in this book was the truth and nothing but the truth get on your computer, I phone, I pad, type in www.karguys.org and vote for the union.

With your votes, we can do it together and get this fucked up corrupted business in the direction that can be fair and correct for everybody.

Chapter ten

CLOSING SUMMARY

'Over 99% percent of car dealers
give the rest a bad name."

IN THE BEGINNING, I SAID THAT I am not writing this book to
become famous among dealers or the dealership employees. I just
wanted to put my voice in print and share the experiences that I have
been through as a car salesman, fleet, internet and finance manager
at different dealerships.

Whether I did a good job or not it is for you to judge but
over all, this little book circles around one very simple point; "pay
your salespeople the commission that was promised at the time of
employment."

You are not paying them what they deserve! At least, don't kink
them, don't pack them, don't bullshit them and most of all, don't
cheat them.

Be a man and honor your word. Don't be a crook, don't be a con
artist, don't be a thief, don't be an asshole and don't be a jack off. Be a

man and do what a real man does. Pay what their pay plan says and let it be fair for everybody.

I do not think that is too much to ask! But since dishonest dealers do not want to stop their kinky habits of screwing the sales people off their time and money, I have no choice but to motivate the car salespeople to unite and vote for the union.

Only union can stop these crooked jackasses from their unfair and unlawful employment practices.

It is shameful that selfishness and greed can take a mans manhood away and change him to a thief and it is unfortunate that we see it happening in dealerships a lot.

Millions of customers have been taken advantage of by dealers in the process of buying, leasing or repairing their vehicles and millions more have been screwed by the same crooked con artist in the name of, "commissioned sales employees."

These weasels have done so many fraudulent acts and have so many skeletons in their closets that hiding things from their salespeople is a must for them. They do not want you to know or see anything. They are paying huge amounts of money from your hard work to their managers to keep it that way.

Every one of these crooks will tell you, "none of what I have written in this book are happening in their dealerships.

These con artists have lied so much for so many years that they don't even know the truth anymore and are drowning in their own lies and bullshit by now.

I do not blame them for trying to hide their unfair ways of doing business which include but is not limited to cheating and stealing from their commissioned sales people. Usually criminals do not admit to their crimes and dishonest dealers are no different.

Salespeople have been seeing it happening to them repeatedly. Unethical practices of dealers are nothing new to the car salespeople. They know it, feel it, sense it, smell it and sometimes even see it, but they cannot say or do anything about it.

Dealers hide everything and if you confront them they will accuse you of not trusting them. They turn the table around to stay on the offensive side knowing that the best defense is a good offense so they can maintain control.

They piss on your back and want you to believe that it is raining. They lie to your face and try to make you believe that you are stupid and don't understand how the auto sales system works.

You want to tell them "you are full of shit" and run to the bathroom and bring out some toilet paper so you can wipe their full of shit mouths. Unfortunately you bite your tongue and say nothing knowing that there would never be enough toilet tissue to clean up their mouths. Their mouths are so full of shit that even their asses get jealous of all the shit that are coming out of there.

The only truth you hear from these con artists is when you are applying for the sales position at their dealerships. The lies and deception starts from the first day telling you everything you want to hear just to get you hired on. They use the same tactics on the salespeople as they do to their customers just to get them in their doors.

They tell you that they are a very fast growing company and if you stay with them you are going to make tons of money and there will be lots of opportunities in the future for you. This one is not a lie and fast growing is the one thing they are being very truthful about.

They are very fast in adding $200 pack on alarm, $300 pack on warranty, inflating the reconditioning cost of used vehicles by $3000, stealing $400 from the front end gross, charging $450 for a non certified used vehicles, $600 regular pack on new or used vehicles and a lot more.

With all of the packing, cheating, stealing, and other kinky shit that they do, they must grow very fast to open dealership after dealership.

Slave driving in car dealerships are a never ending story. We all have heard the old saying of "why buy the cow when the milk is free?"

Lawyers are known for milking their clients but these crooked con artists have been milking their salespeople in the name of commission so professionally and for so many years that even make lawyers wonder.

They have been getting away with not paying wages, salary and the correct and fair commission for so many years that by now it has gone to their fucked up heads and they continue to believe that what they are doing is right.

If car salespeople keep denying about what is happening to them or hoping that a miracle will happen and things are going to get better they must be dreaming.

Miracles do not happen in dealerships and nothing is getting better and in fact, they are getting worse every day that goes by and you are feeling it.

You are working a lot harder, putting in a lot more hours and getting a lot less pay yet still, these lazy crooked assholes are not happy and keep putting more and more pressure on their sales managers and push them to make you put in more hours at their fucking car lots.

Some of these crooks even keep their dealerships open on the Easter, New Years and other holidays.

Some more greedy ones keep their sales departments open until midnight and force their sales team to stay there and make them money. Car dealer and his ass kissing general manager are long gone to bed before their sales department close.

Do you know why? Because the sales people are free slaves and these crooked con artists are slave drivers. Unfortunately there are no laws to stop these greedy jack offs from their kinky and unfair employment practices.

Salespeople do not even notice the weekends and holidays anymore. Weekends and holidays don't mean anything but more hours and more work to the commissioned salespeople in the auto sales industry.

You are working but these con artists are taking off because on the Fridays sales meeting they con you in to it. They throw a little bonus at you to keep you working while they are enjoying their time with their family and friends.

Years ago, a sales manager told me that salespeople are not the only one getting screwed by the dealers, sales managers are getting fucked too. Dealers screw them by inflating the reconditioning cost of the used vehicles and hidden packs that they have on the accessories.

He said "It is the nature of car sales business." Any dealership you go to, the same shit is going to happen and there is nothing we can do about it. That is the way it is and might as well accept it and get used to it.

At the time he was making about $200,000 a year and he knew if the dealer was not stealing from him, he would be making at least another $30,000 or more but since he was very happy with the $200,000 a year, he kept his mouth shut and continued kissing asses and kept stealing from the front end gross of the deals for his asshole bosses.

I will finish this book by asking you please, do not listen to any kind of bullshit or threats from the management. Do not let them sell you or threaten you. We need and must allow the union to step in. In fact we should have had the union over eighty years ago before these scumbags started pulling all kinds of bullshit on us.

Do not accept any "ifs ands or buts" from the dealers. They must accept the union and if they don't then we need to walk out and let these assholes sell their own fucking vehicles, sell their own back end garbage and handle their own fucking heats.

Go to " www.karguys.org" and vote for the union. Do not be afraid of the dealer or his puppet managers. They would never know that you have voted for the union. By having enough vote, we can have unions to protect us from these crooked con artists.

Dishonest dealers, general managers, sales managers and closers can call me as many names as I have called them here in this book. If they think that I give a shit, they can think again.

Sooner or later, we will have strong unions to stop these greedy, crooked, con artist, scumbag and assholes from cheating, stealing and screwing us.

We all know that pay back is a bitch and they are not going to pay us back what they have stolen from us so far, but they just cannot steal from us anymore because the union will be controlling them, just like they have been controlling us.

This book is based on my many years of experience in different car and RV dealerships. It is also based on what I heard from other salespeople at different dealerships.

What you read in this book was the truth, the whole truth and nothing but the truth without any exaggeration or bullshit.

I apologize for being straight forward, blunt and frank about the kinky, crooked and corrupted dealers. Somebody had to do it and I am glad that I am that somebody.

I also apologize for using profanities and I hope my fellow salespeople were not offended by it, but if it offended the crooked and dishonest dealers and their corrupted managements, again, I do not give a shit and neither should you and please remember that I am not doing this for me, we are doing it for us, "the salespeople."

We have all heard not to believe a salesman saying "trust me" but here in the case of having the union, when I say "trust me" I honestly mean it.

I know that I will get bombarded with nasty emails from closers, sales managers and especially crooked general managers and dealers. They can say whatever they want to say.

In this world, everyone has the right to freedom of speech. In some countries you loose that right after you speak but here in America they can keep talking even if they talk shit.

"Over 99 percent of car dealers give the rest a bad name."

Mehdi Roufougar

karguys.com